FROST IN THE ORCHARD

FROST IN THE ORCHARD

Donald R. Marshall

Deseret Book

Salt Lake City, Utah

No part of this book may be reproduced in any
form or by any means without permission in writing
from the publisher, Deseret Book Company,
P.O. Box 30178, Salt Lake City, Utah 84130

Library of Congress Cataloging-in-Publication Data

Marshall, Donald R., 1934—
    Frost in the orchard.

    I. Title.
PS3563.A7213F7   1985   813'.54   85-10252
ISBN 0-87747-916-X

First edition, 1977
Second edition, Deseret Book Company
    First printing August 1985

For Tom
  Mildred
  Monte
  Evalyn
  Barbara
    and Joe

Contents

Christmas Snows,
Christmas Winds

The snow fell today in the streets where trucks and buses spun it into a gray wet spray and left it splattered on parked cars and curbs, pantlegs and soggy shoes; and I feel that it must be falling now too somewhere on the fields and the fence posts, and that somewhere out there tonight when the light turns an icy blue and the dusty snow slithers along the highway like smoke, a black horse standing still in a white field will suddenly shiver and ripple its mane, and maybe a lone figure in coat and overshoes will trudge across that cold expanse with a pail of oats, puffs of steam trailing in the brittle air.

I passed a window where the head of an electric Santa Claus rotated from side to side. Along the crowded sidewalks a loud-speaker blared Fa-la-la-la-la over the muffled heads of passersby. In a crowd on a corner I saw a child licking at a clear red unicorn on a thin stick, and the snowflakes stung my cheeks and burned my eyes.

I remember those glass-candy animals; and I remember other things. I remember the days, the weeks, the months of waiting, interminable hours when December seemed worlds away. I remember tinseled moments even before October's leaves had turned to blue-gray smoke in the November air, when a sudden woody smell of pine or the far-off jingling of a bell sent crystal-shatters of Christmas tingling through my veins. I remember the smell of the new Sears and Roebuck catalogue when it came, and how the pages felt, and how, reaching with some inexplicable power through the endless blur of days ahead, it could steal a handful of Christmas and scatter it instantly, sugared and glittering, before us on the parlor rug where we lay. Every page was Christmas: even a simple plaid bathrobe became magically invested with holly berries and mistletoe, and an ordinary pair of socks triggered immediately a chorus of carolers accompanied by chimes.

I remember the long afternoons at school when the radiator hissed, and bare branches, black against a chalky sky, made soft tapping noises at the windows. Weary of making crayon Christmases on sheets of paper, I would let my pencil plow a little furrow of dirt from the cracks in the floor while I longed for the passing of weeks and waited for that special day. And we would practice the songs for the Christmas program, and I would squirm restlessly on the little painted chairs, excited by the visions conjured by musical fragments—the little town of Bethlehem lying so still with its dreamless sleep and its silent stars, the three kings bearing gifts and traveling from afar, and, perhaps the most glorious of all in those days, jolly old Saint Nicholas leaning his ear and promising not to tell a single soul.

After the endless days of painting and cutting and pasting and shellacking, the secret gifts—plaster of paris plaques or wind chimes of glass rectangles dangling by yarn from a Kerr lid—would lie drying on the low shelves by the radiator, while we filed, in homemade costumes of rabbits or snowflakes, tin soldiers or shepherds, into the little rows of chairs to perform at last before the nebulous faces of relatives and townspeople in the darkened auditorium. "Hark, the herald angels sing!" we chanted, the words to most of the carols garbled even to us, and our minds forever straying to the glossy images in the Sears catalogue. Then the program would be over and there would be no more going back to school for almost two weeks, yet the waiting would go on, only now it would continue in the home—watching from the parlor window for the first sign of a snowflake, carefully printing the letter and trusting it would reach the North Pole in time, studying the blackened flue of the fireplace and wondering how the whole miraculous thing could possibly be brought about.

I remember the days of Christmas-card-making, my materials strewn out on the rug or set up temporarily on a bridge table but inevitably before the fireplace so that I could savor the piney smell and be as near as possible to the popping and crackling fire, its sizzling sap seeming to whisper, "It's coming, it's coming, it's

4

coming!" I recall the snips and scraps of colored paper; the home-made cards with cut-out windows; the obligatory winter scenes drawn laboriously with colored pencils, the village houses and steepled churches somehow owing more to calendar Vermonts than to the Marysvales and Junctions and Circlevilles strung around me.

I remember helping to shake the snow from the tree propped frozen against the porch and running behind as Papa and my brothers dragged it inside through the door, fearing that its branches would be broken and lamenting that its trunk must be shortened. I remember my uneasiness as they grafted boughs in the empty spaces and my surprise and my joy at discovering pine cones and maybe even a bird's nest hidden somewhere in its upper branches. I loved the dusty-sweet and spicy smell loaned by the tree to the parlor; I loved even the sugary pine gum that stuck to my fingers and resisted soap and water, giving way finally only to the salty slipperiness of Mama's butter. And when the dusty boxes were brought up from the basement and opened on the parlor rug, I loved the smell of the candles as we unwrapped them from their crumpled tissue; I loved seeing each tangle of colored lights finally glow against the rug as we tightened every globe and tried each string in the socket to discover which burnt-out bulb was holding back the others; and I loved rediscovering each ornamental bell and ball, old friends momentarily forgotten since that January day nearly a year before when they were wrapped between the Sunday pages of *Maggie and Jiggs* and *Little Orphan Annie* and tucked away in shoeboxes to await December's resurrection. In those days our decorations were a melange of Christmases past and all the dearer for the memories they evoked; almost no ornaments—from the magenta foil cone awaiting candy and nuts to the fragile glass bird with the spun-glass tail—were alike, and the tree lights themselves, many enhanced by metallic reflectors in the shape of water lilies or stars, ranged from a rotund little Santa Claus to an intricate and marvelous Chinese lantern. And when each member of this bizarre menagerie had found a hospitable bough, and when all the foil icicles had been hung until they dripped, silver and shimmering, from almost every needle, we hid the homemade tree stand under a cotton matting, sprinkled it with glistening mica flakes, and set up

5

on its snowy whiteness a miniature cardboard village, a colored bulb in each tiny house glowing softly through a doorway or stained-glass window.

I remember that spicy piney scent suddenly mingling with the smell of whole cloves and cinnamon bark simmering in the hot juices of apples, pineapples, lemons, and oranges that would become wassail to be ladled out in steaming cups for all visitors; and I remember it mingling with the smell of mincemeat pies and rhubarb pies as they bubbled in the oven, and with the smell of doughnuts sizzling in oil, waiting to be fished out and rolled in sugar and eaten hot. I remember peeking over the breadboard as the cranberries and oranges oozed through the grinder to become a sweet relish that tasted like Christmas; I remember the nuts and candied fruit dropping into the spicy batter that would be poured into pans and transformed into golden-brown fruitcakes inside the oven. I remember the annual appearance in the kitchen of figs and dates, an exotic touch of the East that suddenly seemed as right and as welcome as the camel-borne kings parading across our mantel amidst the pine boughs and scented candles.

By Christmas Eve the mound of presents growing under the tree had almost obscured the cardboard village, and each ribboned package there for more than one day had been rubbed and poked and pinched from every angle. But it was what was not there that we waited for most—not the hastily wrapped shapes that would inevitably appear at the last minute on that final eve, but those other things, finally placed unwrapped and glittering in the glow of colored lights, that would never appear until we had eventually drifted off to sleep, with or without visions of sugarplums.

A snowfall on that eve of eves had seemed beyond question, and I remember standing one year in my pajamas looking with incredulity through the window at only a gray-blue bleakness settling in on the dead and naked grass. Santa Claus's sleigh, even flying through the stars, seemed unnecessary and impossible without that obligatory frosty whiteness that had to fall and cover the world. And fall it did. As I pressed a wet cheek against the cold glass, feeling somehow cheated, I saw the first tiny flakes, like lint fluttering in the wind, slithering down the cold blue sky. How necessary it was! In order for the miracle of Christmas to be, the everydayness of mud ruts and frozen gutters *had* to be lost under the sparkling magic of snow.

I remember the snow and I remember other things. I remember the year my stocking hung alone on the string by the fire. My brothers and sisters, suddenly grown away from such things, had turned to dances and caroling atop a horse-drawn hay wagon, and I would peek out of the window into the frosty night, at the faintest rustling of bells, to see them pass or hear them singing above the steady clopping of the mare's hooves on the icy road. From my window, too, I could see down the block to the giant Christmas tree erected in the middle of the town. I could see its lights reflected in the shiny whiteness of the street, and I could watch late shoppers balancing packages as they crept carefully across the ice, calling last-minute wishes to passing friends and then disappearing into the cold night.

I remember lying in my bed under the heavy blankets, wanting to capture every sound—would I hear a tap-tap on the roof or a slithering down the chimney or the clicking of a cup on a saucer as Santa drank the milk and ate the doughnut left for him by the fire?—yet I longed at the same time for sleep to come quickly in order to make the night disappear and the morning come. And when I awoke in the stillness of that blue-violet hour separating night and morning and crept down the darkened hall and through the front room, I always stood entranced on the threshold of the parlor. What other moment could match that moment as I hesitated, scarcely breathing, my eyes taking in the pure magic of each carefully placed and glistening item reflecting the still-burning tree lights and the rosy warmth of the still-smouldering fire, and retaining yet some vestige of the aura surrounding the white-bearded figure whose hand had placed them there—and left only a few sugary crumbs on the saucer by the hearth—perhaps only minutes before?

Careful not to break the spell, I would kneel down quietly to examine, first with my eyes and then with my fingers, each precious piece of a farm set with its hard-rubber pigs and cows, or—another year—a rustic fort with metal Indians and cavalry; once the featured item was a set of Tinker Toys, another time Lincoln Logs, and, still another, a shiny and complicated Erector Set. This was the special

7

hour, that quiet hour before dawn, the room bewitched by the lights of the tree and the only sound an occasional popping of a spark or the soft shifting of coals as the pine logs, now charcoal, crumbled into rose-gold embers. I worshipped this hour, these enchanted moments, when Christmas and I touched, and nothing broke the spell. Even the taking down of my stocking, which now bulged lumpily and heavily on the sagging string, was a ritual. As I turned it upside down, emptying the contents into the lid of a box, I loved every nut, every piece of ribbon candy or multicolored hardtack, even the silver quarter that sometimes rolled down among the cream-centered chocolate Bunker Hills and the inevitable glass-candy Santa Claus or lion or unicorn. There would be an orange, too, and though it was exactly like those colder ones from the kitchen, it seemed marvelous and special; for just as the little nut-covered balls with the cream centers or the pastel-colored sugary mounds were identical to those in bowls on the bookcase, just as each almond and pecan and brazil nut, still in its shell, was no different from those waiting in the wooden bowl with the nut-cracker, each one, like the orange, had been blessed by the hands of Santa Claus, and each one had been chosen and placed there especially for me.

Later on in the morning, when the parlor rug was lost under a storm of wrapping paper and ribbon, we would take turns winding the phonograph to hear Bing Crosby sing "White Christmas" and "Happy Holiday," and the smell of roasting pheasant or duck—shot the day before by one of my brothers—would be drifting from the kitchen while neighbors and uncles and aunts were stomping the snow from their feet outside the door and bursting in, arms full of presents, shouting out the greetings that we all loved. I never tired of showing one more time that marvelous portion of the chaos under the tree that was mine alone, and only in the late late afternoon, when I lay drowsily on the rug before the fire and the house was quiet again, would I feel the melancholy seeping in, the sad sad thought that night was coming on and then it would be tomorrow and tomorrow would be Christmas no more.

But there is something else I remember too. Sometimes I forget it—always I try to forget it—but it keeps coming back like a cold and brittle wind. It claims a part of those Christmas memories too—a part not willed to it or even acknowledged. Unwelcome guest in that memory world of gumdrops and candy canes, it sneaks along the edges of the mind, demanding it be seen, heard, remembered. It is always there, tapping at the back windows like branches in the night.

There was a German family that had a farm a few miles from our town. We scarcely knew them for they spoke little and their English was poor and broken. But we would see them in the town in their faded pickup—the old man with dried manure on his boots, the woman with frightened eyes and a yellowish braid wound around her head. They had a daughter a year or two younger than I, a very quiet girl with pale skin and pale hair, who wore hand-me-downs and moved through the halls of school with scarcely a word. Her English was probably as good as mine, yet we never somehow remembered it that way. We referred to her derisively as Consolation; her real name was Helga or Inger or something like that, but we always called her Consolation because someone, I think, had seen her once with her arm around a child who had hurt his knee on the playground. Sometimes she too wore braids around her head, and then she looked like a strange little mother, grown old before her time. She never had any close friends as I recall, yet we often linked her name, in jest, with anyone we wanted to tease or get back at for something they had done.

One Christmas, when my friends and I were struggling to announce our maturity to the world (no stockings by the fire that year), we slid on the ice and wrestled in the snow outside the schoolhouse until the last cars had driven up in the dark, and the program had already begun with a rousing carol. We then trudged in, during that opening number, and noisily appropriated some empty seats on the front row. We poked each other while the second graders bellowed "Hark, the Herald Angels Sing" in bathrobe-and-towel shepherd costumes, and we traded whispered comments and stifled giggles at the fourth-grade angel with one wing flopping and at Mary with her tinseled halo askew. Then suddenly the junior high band was performing "O Holy Night," and Consolation, we realized to our great mirth, was playing a brief French horn solo. It began wobbly, two or three of the notes were blurbled, and once she even seemed to falter as though she had lost her place. We snickered, and tried, unsuccessfully, to pinch our legs to keep from laughing outright. She finally finished, her frightened eyes, resembling her mother's, dropping to her music stand and never leaving it until the program ended. When it was over and we pushed our way through the crowd outside to where car doors slammed and sputtering engines sent up clouds of white exhaust, we passed by the faded pickup, and I saw the old man there in the dark with his arm around the girl. She was sobbing against the heaviness of his mackinaw, and the woman was soothing her hand over the girl's braids. "Race ya to the corner!" somebody yelled, and we took off, slipping and sliding on the ice and into the night.

Today the snow fell in the streets, and cars slipped and slid and spun around, snarling traffic at every corner. The sidewalks are lost under a gray-brown slush, but maybe the snow will mercifully continue to fall and cover it all. Maybe down the highway where the snow blows like smoke across the road and a lone horse shivers in the wind, the snow will be thick and deep and white. Consolation, where are you now that the snow is falling once again on the fences and the fields? I didn't cry for you then, but I cry for you now.

Friends and Loved Ones
Far and Near/
Merry Xmas from
Our House to Yours

Maxeine and ell :

XMAS GREETINGS FROM OUR HOUSE TO YOURS: 1971
    Thank heavens for such things as ditto machines, when card-sending time rolls around it may not make it quite so personal but it sure beats cramped fingers plus all the expense of store-bought cards that don't hardly give you room enough to say boo. Now if we could just think of a way to get rid of licking all those stamps, ect., ect.

    Our biggest news this year is that I finally got my trip up to Oregon to see Glorene and Norland and their girls. They've been wanting me to come up ever since they moved up there last May. Wiley wouldn't go, he said somebody had to tend to things here at home, so I took the first bus I could get last August and stayed up there over two weeks. Everything was just grand, Norland's fast becoming one of the big wigs there at the plant and sure to be boss of the whole shebang one of these days, they've got them a nice new home just outside Portland, all electric and everything. Of course, they treated me like a queen every step of the way and wouldn't let me pay for a thing. They wined me and dined me day and night and saw to it I got the grand tour of everything there was to see and then some. I wish I could of brought little Janeice and Patsy Ann home with me, they're just so grown-up and ladylike, just like Glorene, but I guess they'll have to wait until next year to see their Grandma.

    Roy Dell and Vergean are still in Frankfurt, Germany, with the army. From the last reports all are doing fine. Roy Dell Jr. is going to the American school there and smart as a whip, just like his dad. I sure wish they'd come home or else I could get over there, but Wiley says he's not going and I guess that's that, although I'd sure like to.

13

RoZann, our baby, is a senior in high school and involved in so many different activities we hardly ever get to see her, I don't know how she keeps it up, playing in the pep band and all.

Come and see us, our doors are always open.

The Lowders of Eureka, Dolpha, Wiley, and RoZann

P.S. Forgot to put in here that Wiley was in the hospital for a week last fall. It was his stomach again but he is almost back to normal. Merry Xmas, Dolpha

FRIENDS AND LOVED ONES FAR AND NEAR: 1971

As the Christmas season draws closer, our thoughts turn once again toward our many dear friends and relatives scattered upon this great land of ours.

We feel indeed blessed this year, grateful for the health and strength that have been ours and ever thankful for the abundance of God's bounty that we have enjoyed throughout the past months.

Our children continue to grow and amaze us all with their many activities and accomplishments. KaeLynn is almost sixteen now, lovely and feminine, delightful to be around, a pure joy to have in the home. Among her many talents are sewing, singing, playing the piano, giving dramatic readings, tutoring the neighbors' children in reading . . . and many, many other things too numerous to tell.

Jolene is thirteen and our little homemaker, winning a blue ribbon for her wool suit in the Orange County Fair last fall. She loves cooking, drawing, music, gymnastics, science, typing, reading, volleyball . . . and, of course, sewing. She is also our newest baby-sitter, so conscientious about this new responsibility and therefore always in demand.

Kevin is our eight-year-old . . . all boy, but such a priceless little spirit. Cars, guns, math, softball, riding a skateboard, and, of course, helping his daddy are among his many interests. He is a regular little scholar as well, winning first prize over all the third graders in the whole school district this last September for his composition on reptiles.

LeMoine is currently engaged in the ambitious task of enlarging the family room and redoing our food storage area. He was number one in sales at work again this year and thus both he and Maccine are anticipating another wonderful trip to either Disney World or Houston, Texas.

Maccine is busy with church and civic activities as usual and finding motherhood more and more fulfilling with each passing day. She is presently enjoying the conveniences of a new dishwasher and water softener and looking forward to an enlarged dining room and extension to the kitchen and laundry room in the not-too-distant future.

Our hearts are full this year as we pause to contemplate our many blessings and to ponder as well the priceless value of friendships and family ties. May this find you all as joyous and blessed as we feel this holiday season. The Shelman Family

P.S. Dolpha and Family: Holiday Greetings and sincere Best Wishes that the New Year may bring many Cherished moments of Great Joy.

Warmly, Maccine

XMAS GREETINGS FROM OUR HOUSE TO YOURS: 1972

Once again here I am with the news from the Lowders in Eureka.

Well, our biggest news is Glorene's divorce. We feel good to have it all over with as it was sure a mess the way it was. The breakup was hard on the girls, Janeice is still just seven and Patsy Ann four and a half, but it's like I told Glorene, it's a darn good thing she got out while the getting was good. Everything was just going from bad to worse. I sometimes think if I could of got up there more often it might not of happened, but I think we're all realizing more and more that it's good riddance to bad rubbage. I could tell things weren't right when I was up there last February, and then when Glorene had to have her cyst operated on in March, I went up again to be chief cook and bottle washer and I told her right then and there I wouldn't of been able to live with him five minutes if it was me. Norland's been a poor loser about the whole thing, fighting

15

every step of the way, but Glorene's got charge of the girls and is determined to keep them—and just as far away from him as she possibly can if any of us have anthing to say about it. I think all that power (he was almost top dog) just went to his head, and, it's like I told Glorene, she just had to put her foot down somewhere. He was neglecting her and the girls and gone a whole lot more than he was ever to home. Poor Glorene's had her hands full, being in and out of court all year, and an operation on top of that, but I tried to get up there as much as I could, and I guess it's finally over and we're all glad of that. For the time being her address is still the same, but I'm trying to get her back down here where we can look after her.

Roy Dell and Vergean are doing just swell, last we heard. They don't write as much as we'd like but I know they all send their love to all of you. You'd think they'd of had enough of Germany by now, but I guess sometimes you have to do what Uncle Sam wants and not what you want.

RoZann, too, probably wishes she was back home here instead of being stuck way up there in Fairbanks, Alaska, where the radio says it's forty degrees below zero, but she and one of her girlfriends got them a chance to work up there for awhile and she claims she's having a good time.

Well, come and see us when you can.

Dolpha and Family

FRIENDS AND LOVED ONES FAR AND NEAR: 1972

Once again, as we approach the Christmas season, we are prompted to recount our multitudinous blessings and to contemplate once more the wealth of friendships and precious family bonds which mean so very very much to us in our daily lives.

Our cup continues to run over. How fortunate we are to have three beautiful healthy children, our lovely home here in Fullerton, another new car . . . now that KaeLynn is of driving age! . . . and so many other blessings too numerous to count.

KaeLynn is a lovely and feminine sixteen, popular and pleasant to be with, a pure delight to have around the home. Not the least among her many interests is music, both instrumental and vocal, followed closely by sewing and reading, not to mention drama, debate, and choral reading.

Jolene is fourteen now and such a joy. In addition to the numerous awards she wins for her sewing, she continues to amaze us with her many other interests and abilities, among which are cooking, typing, reading, music, science, tumbling, swimming, jumping on the trampoline . . . and, of course, babysitting, as she is becoming the most sought-after sitter in the whole neighborhood.

Kevin is our nine-year-old, every inch a boy, but such a help to his daddy and such a pleasant little soul. Among his many interests this year are science, math, machines of any sort, . . . and, of course, softball, wrestling, and sports of any kind.

Besides being honored at work for the fifth straight year, LeMoine keeps busy around the house with his present project being a new carport. We're hoping his company will send us either to Atlanta or Spokane for this year's convention!

Maccine is enjoying working in the home and trying to hold numerous church positions as well. She loves her new kitchen . . . especially the new microwave oven . . . and is hoping Santa will bring her a humidifier this year.

We count your friendship among our most cherished possessions and hope that this new year will bring you great joy and blessings in abundance.

The Shelman Family

FRIENDS AND LOVED ONES FAR AND NEAR: 1973

As we welcome once more the spirit of Christmas into our hearts, we recall the many wonderful blessings that have been ours this year and count ourselves lucky to have among our many cherished friendships such dear close friends as each of you.

Our three lovely children continue to be the source of our inspiration and joy. KaeLynn is almost eighteen, growing more feminine and lovely by the day, it seems. What joy her music brings to us, not to mention her many other talents, among which are such varied things as needlework and the dramatic arts, all of which continue to bring her numerous awards and recognition untold.

Jolene is our little seamstress. When she is not being sought after as the number-one babysitter in the neighborhood, she is busy sewing on countless projects, many of which bring her state-wide acclaim.

Kevin is our ten-year-old this year, such a little man and such a helper to his daddy. He dearly loves school, especially such subjects as math and science and physical education.

LeMoine keeps busy as usual at work and at home, still number one in sales but finding time around the house to do the carpenter work and plumbing. If all goes well, the company will send him . . . and Maccine, of course . . . to either Hawaii or the Bahamas. Wish us luck!

Maccine is still busily working in church affairs and thoroughly enjoying her new living room carpet and drapes.

We want you all to know as the Christmas season approaches how much we think of you and how very important we feel your acquaintance is in our lives. Our wish for the New Year is that you may be even partially as happy and blessed as are

The Shelman Family

XMAS GREETINGS FROM OUR HOUSE TO YOURS: 1974

Here I am a year late. I'm sorry to have disappointed you last year but I was in too much of a dither to even get the ditto typed up, let alone have it run off and stamped, ect., ect.

Well, I was in and out of the hospital a whole lot last year and only got up to see Glorene's family twice. I had a lump that just wouldn't go away and the doctor wanted me to have it taken care of so I did. It turned out to be a hernia and if that wasn't an ordeal! My bathroom was exactly 103 steps down the hall from my room and when you got there the door was so heavy it would just about kill you to try to swing it open. After a week of that, I ended up getting a new hernia and I had to wait another three months for the first one to heal so they could cut me open and start on the other one.

Anyway, I did get up to Idaho a couple of times to help Glorene out, but most of the time I just had to talk to her on the phone. She and her new husband Harlow are still acting like a couple of newly-weds although it has been almost a year now. She is happier than

I've seen her in a long time and of course she's expecting again after all these years which adds to it all. Her finding Harlow was the luckiest thing that ever was as he is everything that Norland was supposed to be and wasn't. And of course I don't mind saying that Harlow's darn lucky to have him a good little wife like Glorene. I went up to be with them this Thanksgiving and left poor Wiley to do for himself (I gave him his choice). They have a nice new home in Boise as Harlow is from there and has him a real good job with a big dried foods company where he's right up there at the top doing most of the hiring and firing. They sent us a whole case of dried okra that's sure come in handy a time or two. He treats Glorene just grand, a real change for her after what she had to go through with Norland. But Harlow is just as good as gold and I sure wish she had run onto him about ten years ago before she ever got mixed up with you-know-who. Harlow has two children, one of each, which they try to get as often as possible. Those little kids of his were just about a nervous wreck when they first got them last summer, but after two weeks you wouldn't of believed the difference, that's how Glorene is, she had them giggling and acting like normal kids in no time. Janeice and Patsy Ann are growing cuter (and more and more like Glorene) every day. Patsy Ann still has a tendency to talk a little baby talk, Harlow thinks they ought to take her to a speech therapist, but I tell him they're only young once and she'll probably outgrow it soon enough. I usually call them up two or three times a week and just love to hear that little voice recite "Twinto, Twinto, Witto Staow" over the telephone, she says it so cute, I just can't imagine her any other way.

Roy Dell and Vergean have been home from Germany for four and a half months now. He is stationed at Fort Devens, Massachusetts, so they don't get to see us much oftener than when they were over there. I want Wiley and me to take one of those tours back there but if I can't talk him into it, I'm going to catch a bus one of these first days and go back there anyway. Vergean says that Roy Dell Jr. is taller than she is now (which isn't saying too much, I guess, as she is practically a midget), but I'm sure anxious to see them and I'd imagine they could use all the help they can get trying to get situated into a whole new place.

RoZann flew back and visited with them in November instead

of coming here for Thanksgiving like we hoped. But I was glad they each had family for Thanksgiving anyway. RoZann liked it so well up in that neck of the woods, though, she got her a job in Nova Scotia and now who knows when she'll get to come home. Seems like we're scattered halfway around the world. Thank heavens Glorene's close. I don't know what she'd of done if I hadn't been able to get up there and help her through some of those bad times. Let's just hope Wiley's stomach doesn't act up and I don't get another hernia so I can be up there to help her out in February when the baby comes.

Our doors are always open.

Dolpha

FRIENDS AND LOVED ONES FAR AND NEAR: 1974

As the year draws to a close and the spirit of Christmas fills our hearts to overflowing, we once again take time from our busy schedules to remember those who are so near and dear to us, and to enumerate the infinite blessings showered upon us this past year.

Not the least among them are, of course, our three dear children—KaeLynn, Jolene, and Kevin. KaeLynn, such a pleasant, lovely, feminine young lady, is going on nineteen, attending college, and continuing to astound us . . . and everyone who knows her . . . with her spectrum of talents, ranging from music to drama to sewing skills.

At sixteen our Jolene is personality plus. Still everyone's favorite babysitter, she somehow manages to find time to win a number of sewing awards. Interested primarily in home economics, she also delights in sports of all kinds, to say nothing of the liberal arts.

Our eleven-year-old Kevin is quite a little grown-up man these days, pleasing everyone with his never-ending wit and knowledge. He loves everything, not the least of which is being with and learning from LeMoine, who continues to be a model father . . . and salesman, of course . . . . at work and at play.

· Maccine is still happily involved with church duties as well as domestic ones, thoroughly enjoying many new additions in the home this year.

Many family excursions and events highlighted the year.

What joy your friendship brings! Again we feel unduly blessed to have, as such an integral and priceless part of our lives, friendships such as *yours*.

The Shelman Family

XMAS GREETINGS FROM OUR HOUSE TO YOURS: 1975

Well, 1975 sure has been a big one. Wiley had to have two-thirds of his stomach taken out and now he has to practically live on baby food. Trying to fix three meals a day that he can manage and still be what help I can to Glorene is a full-time job I wouldn't wish off on anybody. Thank heavens for dried okra, I just boil it down, toss it in the blender, and there you have it.

Glorene and Harlow stopped in just long enough to say hello goodbye last summer on their way home from Disneyland and I got them to take me back up with them to Boise to help out for awhile and still had to go up again three weeks ago when her new baby was born a month early. Kimberly will be a year next month and the baby is just barely three weeks. They couldn't decide on a name, Harlow wanted it Ralph and Glorene had her heart set on Jared. I was a little partial to Jared myself but I finally told them why didn't they name it Jared Ralph and so they did and now Glorene calls it Jared and Harlow calls it Ralph. They're trying to work out a way so that Harlow can adopt Janeice and Patsy Ann, but I don't know what's going to happen because every time Norland gets hold of them he poisons their minds so much they don't think they want to come back. While I was up there during most of August they had Harlow's two with them for awhile so it was your kids, my kids, and our kids for three or four weeks. I was glad I could be there to help out. Harlow tried to talk me into going back to see Roy Dell and Vergean in Maine and RoZann up in Nova Scotia as long as I was up there, offered to pay my way on the bus and everything, and I guess I should of done it while I had the chance but Wiley thought I ought to get back home here and anyway RoZann was talking about maybe going off to Europe with some friends and when I called Roy Dell he said it had been so hot back there all month he couldn't see how I'd enjoy coming back right then, so I still haven't got my trip out there yet.

Roy Dell says they're doing just fine and RoZann says she's still planning to see Europe one of these first days. I'm going to try to get up to Glorene's again after New Year's. She's going to need all the help she can get with those two little babies both in diapers and trying to teach a class every week on fascinating womanhood to boot.

Come and see us if you can, our doors are always open, and in the meantime I'll try to keep you posted on all that's new with the Lowders.

Dolpha

FRIENDS AND LOVED ONES FAR AND NEAR   1975

Christmas 1975 finds us blessed beyond measure, ever mindful of the countless advantages and opportunities which are ours. And once again our thoughts drift toward each of you and the friendship . . . so rich, so choice, so meaningful . . . which we continue to share.

Our little ones, it seems, are ever growing. Our sweet KaeLynn will soon be twenty; she is presently debating between pursuing her career in music or accepting one of numerous proposals . . . ranging from a dashing young law student at Stanford to a handsome executive she met last summer in the northwest.

Jolene is seventeen, so lovely and feminine these days, winning awards galore and being chosen, it seems, for almost every honor imaginable.

Kevin, almost a teenager now, is such a reliable and dependable young man, whose knowledge and abilities never cease to amaze.

Numerous diversions made the year a rich and full one for the Shelmans, LeMoine ever the conscientious breadwinner and Maccine continuing to relish the eternal challenge of managing the home.

If our busy schedules do not permit time for personal notes or if this letter seems shorter than usual, know that our hearts are with *each and every one of you*, as always. May your blessings be even a tenth of those showered in such abundance on

The Shelmans of Fullerton

MERRY XMAS FROM OUR HOUSE TO YOURS: 1976

Thank heavens for these letters once a year, otherwise it wouldn't be possible to keep you all informed on all the activities of the Lowders in Eureka. We're still plugging along here, only I've had trouble with my nose and Wiley seems to be keeping the road hot going up north to see one specialist after another and having his stomach treated.

Glorene, I'm happy to say, finally got out of that mess up there in Boise. She and the girls were here with us for awhile, but she finally got them a little house in Mapleton. Of course I wish they would of stayed here with us but Wiley seems to be showing his age a whole lot more than I am and I guess having the kiddies around twenty-four hours a day would get on his nerves, ect., ect. I try to get over there three or four times a week, though, as the kids need to see their Grandma and Glorene of course needs all the help and moral support she can get. Thank heavens she doesn't have to put up with those two of Harlow's any more. I wish all of you could see Glorene's four though, every one of them just as pretty as a picture. The oldest two put me in mind so much of Glorene herself when she was their age. Of course, she hasn't changed a whole lot herself. Janeice is the babysitter now, already thirteen and going to be just like her mother. And little Patsy Ann, such a doll, is becoming quite the little lady. Now it's little Kimberly who's the thumbsucker, Patsy Ann's just about given it up, and little bitty Jared has got the cutest set of curls you've ever seen. I hope she never has to cut his hair, he puts me in mind less of Harlow (thank heavens) than of how little Roy Dell Jr. used to look before they cut off all his hair and he started traipsing off to the ends of the earth so we hardly ever see them at all. RoZann seems to be taking after them, she's got her a job as a stewardess and seems to fly everywhere you can think of but Eureka.

Well, hope your year has been a little cheerier than ours, although things are looking a whole lot brighter now that I've got Glorene close to us here. Harlow still gives her a lot of trouble, he's worse than Norland for that, but if I have my way, he won't get within a mile of her or those kids. Glorene still feels kind of blue once in a while, but I tell her, looking as young and cute as she still does, it won't be long before someone falls for her, I just know it. She's had a couple of raw deals but we're still in there rooting for her.

Until next year,

The Lowders of Eureka
Dolpha,
Glorene,
and Wiley

FRIENDS AND LOVED ONES FAR AND NEAR: 1976

As we stand on the brink of this promising new year, we look back with thanksgiving in our hearts for the multitude of blessings that have been ours, not the least of which is the wonderful kinship and friendship we share with so many dear friends and loved ones so frequent in our thoughts and so close to our hearts though, in most cases, so very far away.

The blessings and responsibilities of the Shelmans continue to increase as our family begins to branch out and grow, for KaeLynn is now Mrs. N. J. Marchant (pronounced Mar-*shawnt*) of Seattle, Washington, where her husband is vice-president of Miller-Marchant Associates. Maccine is looking forward to visiting the Marchants in their lovely new home in the very near future.

Jolene, as busy as ever, is faced with the dilemma of going on to college to become a fashion design expert or choosing one of several other . . . equally attractive . . . alternatives.

Kevin is all teenager, a real thinker, with a mind of his own, forever a joy whenever he is present.

Our lives continue to be rich and full, always a challenge. This has been such an eventful year in the Shelman household, LeMoine forever seeking new opportunities and Maccine busier than ever at home and working on various projects.

May we impress upon you our sincere best wishes for the coming year. Our lives would be so empty without the many dear and cherished friendships which so enrich our daily lives despite the miles that separate us. Season's greetings to one and all from

The Shelmans

The Thorns

She had seen the sign, DAY-CARE CENTER FOR THE AGED, through the mud-splattered blur of the windshield shortly after she had turned onto the highway, and the glaring yellow letters seemed to have burned themselves into the back of her retina so that they continued to taunt her—and tempt her—as she moved later among the rows of canned soups and glossy tomatoes, numbly checking off the items on her list; and they were still there, yellow and glaring, even after she had put the last bag of groceries into the car and started back up the road while whirring traffic spewed wet brown snow across the windshield.

When she passed the sign for the second time, LaRuth let the car creep through the slush alongside the road while she strained to peer through the gray-streaked side window to the place beyond the sign where the old house with its pillared porch and dripping eaves sat soggily in a scrap of thin snow and brown grass. "Somebody must have bought the old Widtsoe home and fixed it up," she told herself aloud, as she pulled back onto the road, still frowning. She would need to find out more about it, that was sure, but it *was* something to think about. It was, in fact, something she couldn't cease thinking about; and it both annoyed and excited her.

She would tell Verl about it, that's what she would do, and maybe he too would see it as some sort of an answer. And it *was* an answer, wasn't it? It wouldn't be as though they were sending him off to a rest home to dwindle away his years among strangers. Not that he would know any more people here than at the homes she had checked into in Logan and Ogden; Brigham City could never be for the old man what Coalville had been for him. But at least there wouldn't be that sense of finality here that must have bothered Verl when she had told him about Braithewaite House and Logandale and the others. If it really were a day-care center, then it would be ideal, wouldn't it? It would just be for a few hours a day, maybe from eight to four or from nine to five, and he would always have the knowledge that she and Verl were not giving him up, that they were in no way cutting him off from the family, but that there would always be someone there every evening to pick him up and bring him home with them.

But maybe it wasn't ideal, after all. It was usually not during the day that was so bad. It would still leave unresolved the problem of the bedrooms: she flinched when she thought how, despite their careful plans for two bedrooms so that each child might have his own, Stevie and the baby had been inconveniently crowded into one room ever since Verl's father had been thrust suddenly upon them. And it was the suppertime that bothered her most, wasn't it? —the uncomfortable suppers with his wheezings and coughings and snortings and endless repetition of personal anecdotes that had long lost their capacity to amuse. But at least at suppertime Verl would be there to help her share the burden.

As soon as he came home she would tell him about it. If he couldn't quite bring himself to consider a permanent rest home for his father, then wouldn't this be just the thing? She would have to ask the operator if there was a new listing for a day-care center and then find out how much it would be for such an arrangement, but it sounded like an almost perfect solution. And it shouldn't end up being much more trouble than it was dropping Stevie off for school or—as she had done this afternoon—dropping the baby off at Hilma's for an hour or two. It was something to think about at least, and she felt anxious to share the new idea with Verl.

She had planned on stopping home to put a few things in the freezer before picking up the children, but when she turned up her street and saw the faded maroon car still in the driveway, she decided to risk letting the broccoli and the cherry-nut ice cream thaw out on the back seat and drove instead on toward the schoolhouse. Erna Mae and Woodrow or Woodruff or whatever her husband's name was had called earlier to say they were passing through

on their way back to Coalville from Idaho Falls and could they stop
a minute or two to say hello to Clovis, but she had assumed that
they would have come and gone in all the time she had been gone to
the supermarket. Verl's father, she knew, was pleased they had
thought about him, and she too had been relieved that there would
be someone there to keep him company for part of the time she
would be away shopping, but it did surprise her that they were still
there. It wasn't that she didn't like Erna Mae or *that* part of Verl's
family; it was just that she had only met them once or twice and
always felt at a loss for something to talk about. Besides, if they were
really only second or third cousins to Verl's father, what would that
make them to her? She had clearly never grieved over the fact that
there were first cousins of her own in Rock Springs, Colorado, and
also somewhere in Nebraska whom she had never even met, yet
Verl's father would frequently interrupt his morning ritual of reading the daily obituaries to announce to her that the second or third
cousin of so-and-so who was married to the second or third cousin
of so-and-so and used to live in Coalville back in the twenties or
thirties had dropped dead of a heart attack in Missoula, Montana,
or some other such place, and the look in his eyes then would be so
hopelessly forlorn that it always made her feel as though he
expected the bottom to have dropped out from under her world too.
What did he think it could possibly mean to her that someone
named Alonzo Nielson, age 83, had died last week in Snowflake,
Arizona?

  She was disturbed then, when, having picked up coughing
Stevie and wiped his nose and scolded him for running around with
his coat unbuttoned, then having stopped by Hilma's to pick up the
baby and carry her bundled up in the collapsible car bed to share
the back seat with the bags of groceries, she drove once again by her
house twenty minutes later and found the maroon car still parked in
the driveway. It annoyed her too that she had to park on the road—
and that the snowplow that morning had bequeathed her a small
barricade of slush, the color of dirty dishwater, between the road
and her own sidewalk—and it was not until she had lifted Stevie
over the mound and turned back to the car to fumble with the
groceries and the car bed that she heard someone call from the front

door, "Oh, that's a rotten shame you had to park clear out there. Let us get out of your way and you can pull right up here in the driveway."

With a bag of groceries in each arm, her purse clutched in one hand and the car bed handle gripped in the other, she managed to step over the melting snowbank and onto the sidewalk with only one shoe soaked and nothing more than a box of Krispy Kritters toppling onto the wet cement before they were there—all three of them—blocking her path in their well-meant confusion. "That's a dirty shame," Erna Mae was saying, relieving her of the car bed, giving her a little squeeze around the waist, and passing out directions all at once. "How are you anyway, hon? Wilford, get that car door for her, would you, and see if there's any more to bring in? Have we got it all? Oh, and isn't that baby just the cutest thing you ever saw! What do you call her? I swear if you'd of been a minute later we'd of been gone. I was just telling Wilford we'd better get on the road if we're going to beat that storm in the north. But I'm glad we got to see you anyway even if it is just for a minute. You world travelers—was it Afghanistan where you was that time? Let me hold that door open—can you get that, Clovis? Oh my, and look at this little man! Don't he look like his Daddy, though—and a school boy and everything!"

By the time she reached the kitchen, LaRuth was exhausted, even though they had relieved her of all but one sack and her purse. Erna Mae was kissing the baby and repeating "ah-boo, ah-boo," while her husband maneuvered the rest of the groceries through the doorway, and the old man and Stevie disappeared into the front room. Without taking off her coat, LaRuth searched out the sack with the ice cream and frozen vegetables and said, "Excuse me long enough to get a couple of these things into the freezer—"

"Listen"—Erna Mae was there giving her arm a little squeeze—"don't you worry about fixing anything for us for one minute. We should of gone an hour ago. I told Wilford, I said"—and suddenly her voice dropped to almost a whisper—"we almost never come at all it was getting so late and that storm coming on from up north just as sure as you're born, but"—her grip on her arm tightened and her voice dropped so low that LaRuth had to stop putting the broccoli in the freezer and look at her—"I'll tell you one thing, I wouldn't of missed seeing him for all the world and that's a fact. And I think he was just as tickled to see us as we was him. I told Wilford, I said, I don't care if it's five minutes to say hello – good-bye or if it's an hour or two, but I couldn't no more see passing through Brigham City and not see him than fly to the moon." Erna Mae didn't release her grip, but her eyes narrowed and her voice dropped even lower still. "He's not long for this world, we all know that, with him being eighty years old or better. I'm surprised to see him here this winter at all, if you want to know the truth. But I'll tell you one thing"—and here she pronounced each word slowly and earnestly, accompanied by an almost imperceptible yet deliberate shaking of the head—"he's the grandest person that ever lived."

For a moment there was nothing but silence and Erna Mae's eyes, moist and penetrating. Then the grip loosened, Erna Mae finally sighing and saying, "Well, anyway, I'm glad we come," and LaRuth was relieved to go back to putting away the broccoli.

"From the looks of that sky, Wilford," Erna Mae's voice came from the other room, "we're going to get caught right square in the middle of a blizzard if we don't get on the road right now."

"—better get back down there and see if Garn's done his chores—" Wilford was saying.

"Bye, honey," Erna Mae waved in through the doorway, her husband smiling, nodding, and following suit behind her. "Sure wish we could of seen Verl."

LaRuth managed to fake a smile. "He'll be sorry he missed you." She felt vaguely grateful that there were no mirrors in the room, thankful to be spared the added discomfort of having to watch herself play an unwanted role and play it badly.

She did not have to play it long. "Mommy, Mommy, my nose!" Stevie was calling, his face upturned and contorted to display the effects of a violent sneeze, and she clutched up the baby from the old man, grabbed Stevie by the hand, and nodded an apologetic farewell as she almost dragged him up the stairs, her relief at being able to leave them to their own good-byes far exceeding any embarrassment she might have felt. The nose wiped, she did not bother to go down again, even though the draft up the stairs and the continuing muffled voices below told her they still lingered in the doorway. Bits of voices drifted up the stairwell: "—well I think you're looking just grand" and "—I still think about them biscuits you made up at the reservoir that time—" She cringed; the old man always called it *rez-a-voy*.

When at last she heard a faint cough and then the awaited click of the door followed by receding voices, she slipped into the bedroom, the baby against her chest and Stevie at her side, and stood by the curtains looking down into the snow-covered yard where she could see the three of them, linked arm in arm, moving slowly down the icy walk. A cold wave rippled through her. It was like an optical illusion, like a familiar name or word that suddenly glares back at you with a defiant unfamiliarity, having shifted with the blink of an eye to become something strangely new and alien. From where she watched, the old man now seemed to have taken on a different appearance. She saw him daily—not daily, *hourly*; every minute, in fact, it seemed that he was there somewhere under her feet—shuffling down the hall behind her, talking to himself or mumbling aloud the obituaries at the kitchen table while she cooked, snoring and making funny noises in his throat while she mended clothes or watched TV. She had tried to live her life in spite of him, had tried, in fact, to almost ignore him, to move around him as though he were another piece of furniture, something bequeathed but unrequested. But it had not always been easy. She watched him now through the curtains, and the strange wave splashed through her again. Seeing him there, taller than either of the two supporting him down the walk, looking not shriveled now but strangely straight and towering, his white hair lifted and blowing in the wind, she felt almost as though she were seeing him for the first time.

She moved back uneasily from the window, then looked through again. It was as though the scene below were trying to tell her something, but she was not sure what it was. Then she remembered. She would have to tell Verl about the sign she had seen telling about the day-care center.

"Mom! Mom-m-MY!" Stevie was tugging at her hand for attention. "Will you try to find them now? Remember?" She felt as if she were waking up suddenly in a strange room, and her look must have betrayed her bewilderment, for he went on impatiently, "The valentines!"

The valentines. She had promised. She put the baby on the bed and knelt by the cedar chest. Opening it, even after all these years, was still a ritual: first came the spicy smell of the cedar wood, and with it the inevitable memories of pink and white mints, fuchsia-tinted lemon slices floating in a crystal punchbowl, and Leona Brinkerhoff singing "My Hero" from *The Chocolate Soldier*. The mints were fact, she knew that; but she also knew that, in actuality, there had never been any lemon slices in the punch that day nor Mrs. Brinkerhoff's vibrato rendering of "My Hero" beside the upright piano. (It had been Laura Lee Wilcox instead, she remembered, singing "The Twelfth of Never.") Yet she rejected none of these "borrowed" memories, but embraced them warmly, for they were in there too, a definite and inextricable part of it all, through relics from the trousseau teas of others—of older sisters, sisters-in-law, aunts, and cousins there in Brigham City.

"Are they in *there?*" Stevie asked, one finger touching the white textured cover of her wedding book. "Just wait," she cautioned, carefully removing his hand for him. Next came the satin pillow-cases and the linen ones with pink tatting on the edges—too elaborate for use, too old-fashioned for her taste, yet somehow too precious to ever give away. Next the reversible peach and sherbet-green quilt her mother's friends had quilted for her, then the baby books—Stevie's and then the new one for Angie. Embroidered dish towels followed, along with damask table cloths and napkins—unused and now made obsolete by permanent-press fabrics, yet still too beautiful to part with. Next, in a box that she did not open now, was one of her earliest dolls, its hair matted and one eye lodged crookedly in its head, cushioned with stacks of homemade doll clothes; beside it was a maroon velvet watch case containing her senior-class ring and seminary pin, and, under that, a sagging shoe-box held together with string and rubber bands where she kept two of her own baby dresses, a yellowed undershirt, and a pair of discolored booties.

Her eye caught the bold print on a newspaper wrapped around some photographs: ART TREASURES MUTILATED. She skimmed the column—someone had secretly gouged with scissors the eyes and faces of several valuable paintings in the Uffizi Gallery in Florence, Italy. The newspaper was old, but she recalled with a shiver how someone had not so long ago disfigured with a hammer Michelangelo's famed *Pieta*. As her eyes began to flit greedily over the other columns partially visible on the scrap of old newspaper, she wondered why it was that such bits of news always became more fascinating when discovered on the kitchen floor after she waxed it, or paint-spattered under a half-refinished stool, or even, years later, glimpsed in the bottom of a dresser drawer.

"Is that the one?" Stevie was pointing now at the brown scrapbook on top of the stack of photo albums and BYU yearbooks. "That's it," she said, taking it up, her mind already turning through the pages of randomly organized memories, anticipating the photograph of herself and of her roommates as they had posed on the steps of the Maeser Building that first fall, tossing back their ponytails and raising their calf-length skirts to display a knee; Verl in his dinner jacket, she in her ballerina-length formal with the gardenia on her wrist at the Fieldhouse Junior Prom; and, later, their skirts shorter and their hair styles borrowed from Liz Taylor and Natalie Wood, she and her Val Norn sisters radiating around their hard-earned Song Fest trophy. Near the back, in pages not long ago still blank, they found the valentines: homemade ones with glitter and paper doilies, five-for-a-penny ones with sentimental messages printed in pencil by grade-school lovers; expensive ones—"To my darling," "Sweetheart," "All My Love"—some from Verl and some from a boy she scarcely remembered; and then the old ones: one, found recently among her mother's things, with a red satin heart-shaped sachet that still carried a faint scent, and one that her mother had long saved (from *her* mother perhaps?), yellowed and brittle now around its Victorian edges, its cherubs, winged and ladened with garlands, bordering a wistful woman, all Virtue and Motherhood, in her Gibson upsweep and high lace collar.

Voices, faint yet distinct outside the window, brought her back to the palpable present of the warm room and Steven breathing bronchially beside her. Still kneeling, she shifted the weight of the book to the boy's lap, and straightened herself to look out through the curtains. It irritated her that they were still there standing on the sidewalk; Verl's father's cough was sure to be worse. She watched them all embrace, Erna Mae patting the old man's arm and reaching up to peck at his cheek while her husband grasped the old fellow's hand in both of his and held to it while he said something she couldn't hear. Still clinging, the three of them moved slowly toward the car, then stopped, exchanged smiles and nods and un- heard words, then, surprisingly, reenacted the whole procedure once again—the hugs, the kisses, the clasping of hands, the nods. It was strange how absurd and ridiculous people seemed when their trivial actions, viewed out of earshot and from a vantage point like hers now, were transformed into a clownlike pantomime. She watched them now, Erna Mae pausing once again to pat the old man's arm and nod before she got into the car. And she watched him bend to wave at the hands waving back vigorously through the windshield as the car backed into the street. For a moment the car seemed to stall; then she saw it quiver and sputter forth a cloud of heavy white exhaust, and the exaggerated waving resumed. A pickup came down the street—again they waited—but when it turned the corner, the waving began once more in renewed earnest- ness and continued until the maroon car was lost from sight and the old man turned back toward the house. LaRuth touched her fingers to the smile still hovering on her lips. If people could only see themselves, she thought; and she could hold back the smile no more.

When she went down later to start the supper, she found him asleep at the kitchen table, his glasses almost slipping off his nose as he snored, the newspaper, spread open to the obituaries, dangling off his lap. He was blocking the way between the stove and the refrigerator again, and she found herself rubbing the knuckles of her hands as if to warm them and thinking how desperately she had to talk to Verl. Finally she said, "Grandpa—" and he stirred, blinking behind his glasses, and wiping a large palm across his mouth where a drop of saliva had been about to drip. "Just reading here—" he said fuzzily, fumbling for his papers.

"I didn't mean to wake you," she said in the louder-than-normal tone she felt she had to use with him, "but I think maybe you'd feel better if you—"

"Oh, I wasn't asleep," he protested, adjusting his glasses and running his hand over the newspaper to locate where he had left off. "I was just reading here where Clair Willis's boy died of cancer down in Phoenix—"

She turned to the sink. It infuriated her how he never admitted to sleeping; he was always just resting his eyes, he said, or just thinking about something.

"—don't know if you ever met any of LaMon Dutton's girls," he was saying, "but the oldest one—Rita Jean, I think they called her—was married to—"

She turned on the hot water tap and his voice was lost momentarily as the water drummed and rumbled into the dishpan. No, she did not know them, nor did she feel that her life was any less rich because she had not. She found unbearably tiresome his incessant recounting of names and their inevitable linkings with names of second and third cousins.

"—and Verl and Keith J. and all of them would go down there, not a one of them a bit bigger than little Stevie, and they'd stay the whole day riding the horses and helping LaMon water his pasture and—"

She stared at the water in the sink, wondering why she had drawn it. Outside it had already grown dark, and she watched anxiously through the window above the sink as two car lights passed slushily by. Her hands had discovered a head of lettuce and she found her fingers tearing impatiently at the leaves.

"—when Keith J. come home, I asked him where he got that bridle from, and he hemmed and hawed around a minute or two and then looked up at me and—" The old man started to laugh a little here as she knew he would, as she knew he always did when he reached that part in the story. Her fingers tore almost wildly now at the lettuce leaves. " 'But Daddy,' he says to me"—and the old man interrupted himself again with a series of little chuckles back somewhere in his throat—" 'Daddy,' he says—"

The lettuce was nothing but leaves now, and there were only her own cold hands pulling at one another, and she felt as if she were going to scream.

Then, two lights turned into the driveway and Verl was home.

During supper she listened to the clinking of forks against the plates. Stevie's cold seemed to be worse, and she watched him as he poked, snuffling and watery-eyed, at the Pakistani casserole that she knew he liked. She was aware too that, beside her, the old man had not even touched with his fork the small portion she had given him, but instead, had noisily eaten three helpings of creamed potatoes. She had not expected that he would eat the casserole. He couldn't chew beef or eat pinenuts, the vinegar always disagreed with him, and she knew he found the cumin seasoning strange. She had been aghast at the abundance of things he could not eat, and shocked further still at the foods— almost any vegetable, it seemed, other than basic corn, peas, and potatoes—with which he claimed no familiarity at all, items that she was finding she liked more and more. If he wanted to be a part of the family, it seemed to her that—

"Got any more of that rabbit food tucked away back there?" Verl was asking across from her, twisting around in his chair at the same time to where she had left the bowl of salad on the kitchen counter. Watching him generously serve himself, she stirred uneasily. The old man, she suspected, would not eat much of that either, finding the cauliflower too difficult to chew, the green peppers and onions too hard on his stomach, the salad seasoning too intense. She looked at Verl as he ate. He too had seemed to look at her two or three times during the meal as if there were some message she was supposed to be receiving. Maybe he too, she thought with a sudden surge of excitement, had seen the new sign on the highway.

Beside her the old man was keeping Stevie from eating as he mumbled something about a wagon overturning into an icy creek. She stopped listening; it would be the story about his stepmother or his mother's stepsister or whoever she had been and how she had been trapped under the wagon all night, or maybe it would be the story of the lady—also some relative or another—who had dragged her husband or brother out from under a wagon and carried him on her back up onto the road or to the nearest cabin or whatever. She had heard them all a thousand times, it seemed. She was not even sure the old man kept them straight. How could he, when he could not even remember simple things anymore, like where he had put his glasses or his newspaper or whether anyone had telephoned while she had been out. She had always suspected his vision of things: while they had lived in the East and Verl was finishing graduate school, the old fellow had written to them regularly: "The town is growing so you'd hardly know it," he would write of Coalville, naming the people who had moved in, the houses being built, the gas stations going up. But his mother's letters, the words round-ly yet minutely formed in pencil, had seemed more accurate: "The town is dwindling," she would write. "Everyone is moving away. So many houses closed up. None of the young people stay here any more." And she was sure his vision of the past was clouded and dis-torted. It annoyed her, in fact, to hear him still go on talking about the Hepworths and the first sawmill or the first hotel or whatever it had been in Emery County. He talked about his link with those first settlers—relatives, in some remote way, of his mother's side of the family—as though he were claiming kinship with some ancient line of kings or nobles. The last time he had gone on about them, naming each one and some tie-in or association each had had with Brigham Young or Parley Pratt or whoever, she had wanted to break in and ask him to produce some sources, to provide some sort of verification or documentation. Once, shortly after they had re-turned West from graduate school and from their stay in Pakistan, they had asked him what they could get him for Christmas, and he had told them how he had been looking for years for a good history of Utah that would tell about his ancestors, those famous Hepworths, and the important part they had played in settling of the area around Emery County. Relieved to be free of the burden of selecting once again the perfunctory shirts, ties, or socks, she had earnestly tried to locate the sort of book he wanted, and a bookstore in Salt Lake had finally, after several weeks, produced one for her. But there had been no Hepworths mentioned in it. The book was still upstairs in some closet.

"Anyone here interested in seeing any slides of Pakistan to-night?" Verl broke in.

LaRuth quickly glanced over at Stevie who, still staring intently at his grandfather as the old man went on about the wrecked wagon and the horse that had to be shot, had fortunately not heard the inquiry, and then she looked back at Verl to scold him with her frown. Not quite sure whether it was her own headache or more altruistic motives that prompted her, she tipped her head toward Steve and mouthed emphatically to Verl the words, "He's got to get to bed!"

"—and it wasn't clear until the next morning before anybody else came along that trail," the old man was saying. She frowned

36

again and poked at the cold remainder of the casserole left on her own plate. It had relieved her that Stevie had not heard Verl's question, but it irritated her at the same time that the old man also had not heard, that he had gone on with his own story as though it were the only thing that mattered within that little room. Although at times it seemed a blessing, it still bothered her that he seemed to hear so little. His talking to himself occasionally as he shuffled around from room to room made her uneasy, but his not hearing was often a nuisance. She suspected now that, even if the old man had heard the invitation to see the slides of Pakistan, he would have countered with something about Coalville or wagon wheels or sawmills. He seemed so rarely to take an interest in any of their things, to make an effort to become a part of their family.

They had done their best. She had never forgotten that fall six years ago—Verl's last year at Boston U.—when, after the birth of Stevie, his parents had finally been persuaded to make the big trek eastward to visit them. It had not been what she would like to think of as "a pleasant experience," although she was glad that they had finally come since Verl's mother, unknown to them at that time, must have already had gnawing away inside her the cancer that eventually took her life before their second child was born. She thought of the woman now—and not without a tinge of uneasiness, for, from the first weekend Verl had taken her home to Coalville, she had preferred the big man with the white hair who had clasped her hand in his massive warm one to the little sharp-nosed lady with bronze hair who had scrutinized her through pointed rhinestoned glasses. She thought of her now and saw her just as she had been that October afternoon in Boston—her pink-orange hair with its grey roots and hundreds of tiny pin-curls held down by an invisible hairnet; her pink chiffon scarf and fur collar catching the too-pale powder on her neck; her lips, painted redly and unevenly, sucking inevitably on a mint. Standing beside her in his gray overcoat that seemed too small and too old, he had looked like a farmboy dumped on the corner of a great alien city; but both had looked equally lost ˌand out of place. She remembered how she and Verl had taken them to see the glass flowers at Harvard, and it angered her now as much as ever to recall how they had given them adequate directions and dropped them off near the library and then been incensed when they went to pick them up an hour or so later to discover that they had never gone inside. She had blamed Verl's mother at the time—she who had insisted on making the trip eastward by bus instead of by air because the planes frightened her—but she had come to realize, since the woman's death, that the old man was perhaps even less a tourist than his wife had been, that he had no intention of breaking loose from his provincial mold. Traits that had once been mildly amusing from afar had now, in these nine months since the selling of the Coalville homestead and the old man's coming to live with them, become irritating thorns that pricked her and tore at her.

The old man had turned toward her and was saying something about the year they had had so much fresh corn they didn't know what to do with it. He had a smear of white sauce on the corner of his mouth and she recoiled. Why wasn't he aware of that? Then her eye caught the thing that always repelled her most of all. One long, almost colorless hair protruded from one of his nostrils. She swallowed and felt thankful for the second time that day that there were no mirrors in the room. She tried to eat but felt that she had to look at him. Stop talking about the corn, she wanted to blurt out. Stop talking to me about the farm, and about Keith J. and Liddie and Arvis. Stop talking about Coalville, and the year of the big drought, and the good harvest of '27, and the heavy rains, and the crickets, and the combine, and the grain. How can you sit there and talk at all, she wanted to cry out, with that sauce dribbling from your lips and that grotesque white hair sticking out of your nose!

She found herself suddenly nodding quickly and almost overturning the chair as she got up from the table. At the sink she tried to calm herself as she stood, her back to the others, running hot water over the dirty plate and the glass snatched up hurriedly as she had mumbled something about dessert and left the table. And when she opened the refrigerator to get the ice cream, she let herself remain motionless for a few seconds before the open door, the frosty air cooling her arms and cheeks.

When she came down the stairs later, most of the tension that had earlier hummed inside her like a fluorescently flickering neon light had burned itself out, leaving her with an overwhelming sense of exhaustion. The baby had gone down fretfully, and Stevie, not mistaking the sound of the portable movie screen being removed from the hall closet, had evidently sensed some activity under preparation downstairs from which he was excluded, and he had begged, as a compensation, an extra story. She hesitated on the stairway as the light from the living room went out, leaving only a dim glow from the slide projector to illuminate the hallway. She could see the old man moving about, mumbling, in the front room. He would be looking for his glasses. Through the door to the kitchen the haphazard stacks of dirty dishes waited beside the sink. Two evils, she thought, and she surprised herself by choosing the darkened room where familiar streets of Karachi flashed in rectangles against the screen and the old man was now clearing his throat and coughing in the corner. Maybe there would be a moment, if he left the room or fell asleep, when she could tell Verl what she had seen.

"Have you seen all of these, Dad?" Verl's voice came out of the dark as the picture changed.

"What's that?"

"Have you seen these before?"

"I suspect so. But don't worry about me." He seemed to be fidgeting with the pillows on the couch, making himself comfortable. "You just go on with your sorting or whatever it is you got to do, and I'll just sit back here and—"

"Did I ever show you this? That's Achmet and the guy on the left is Abdul, the one who had worked with me on the Rawalpindi project. That gray building—"

"You say you took these with that camera we gave you for graduation?"

She was offended—for Verl. The little old box camera that Verl had come across in a box after they were married had been given to her to use for a while, but when a repair man had told them that fixing the faulty shutter would exceed the worth of the camera, it had long ago become a part of the odds and ends in Stevie's toy box.

"Nah," Verl was saying, changing the slide. "You've seen that camera Keith J. got me in Korea, haven't you? Look at this one. Did you ever see a woman carrying a load like that?"

The old man didn't respond. Another picture flashed on the screen.

"This was just around the corner from where we worked every day on that last project. Look at that guy by the window, Dad. They used to break their legs or tie their arms and legs back when they were little to purposely deform them. There's a law against that now." The picture changed. "And look at this. That little girl had been brushing her teeth with her finger right there in the mud on the street."

She could see the old man shifting restlessly in the dark.

"Did you see this one, Dad? Remember that, LaRuth?" She saw an old man with his hand-propelled sewing machine working on a white cotton tunic in the dirt before a mud hovel. She could not have named the exact time or even the village but the scene came back to her—accompanied now by the memories of smells and sounds—with the familiarity and strangeness of a dream. She glanced at the old man, dimly illuminated in the projector's light, to see if he were asleep. He was leaning forward on the couch as if preparing to say something. The slide changed.

"Look at that, Dad. That's the kind of places they live in. Every day we—"

The old man made a little noise in his throat and inched forward on the couch. "I should think," he suddenly announced rather loudly and emphatically, "that you would have had your fill by now of all the poverty and ugliness you'd ever want to see without thinking of dragging LaRuth and those two babies of yours down into Guatemala like you said the other day—"

"I just mentioned that maybe—"

"If it's beautiful scenery you want, you don't need to drive twenty miles. There's not a prettier place in the world than—"

"Come on, it's not just the scenery," Verl tried to say, but his father was not listening.

"—and it would cost a darn sight less, I can guarantee you that." The old man was standing up. "If you want to see pretty scenery, instead of a lot of those—"

This time she broke in. "We loved Pakistan. I loved everything about it," she lied. "And if we can work things out"—thoughts of Keith J. and Verda and the day-care center tumbled upon her—"we would love to take another trip, whether Verl's company will send us or whether—"

Verl had turned around in his chair and was touching her arm. Obeying his signal, she stopped, leaving her sentence unfinished. But her mind went on: yes, she would actually welcome Guatemala. She would welcome anywhere. When Verl first mentioned it, months before, the idea had fallen upon her like an unexpected burden, and she had balked at the vision of traveling this time with running noses and dirty diapers, of boiled water and cold showers. But suddenly it looked like a way out. It was an escape from a greater burden she could not bear, and she welcomed it.

Verl had turned off the projector and switched on the pole lamp. The old man paced before them.

"I never had any desire to hunt out other people's poverty," he was saying. "If it's ugliness you want, you can find it without gallivanting halfway around the world to look for it. But I always said—"

She didn't want to hear more. She didn't care what he always said. He would never be able to understand their lives and what was important to them. She started for the kitchen.

"Sit down here, LaRuth," the old man was saying. "Let me find that box of slides I took on the Yellowstone trip. If you want to see—"

She cringed. Although she could not remember them, she knew what they would be: an endless series of slides bought at the lodge's souvenir counter, poorly reproduced in an inevitable nebulous shade somewhere between orange and lavender; and others, snapped by the old man himself—blurry and tilted shots of Keith J. feeding the bears and Grandma in her coat and hat standing in front of Old Faithful.

"I can show you some real scenery," he was saying, "if I can find those pictures I took that time in the Tetons. There's no more beautiful thing in all the world than—"

From upstairs the baby cried out, and she felt mercifully spared. "Let me see what's wrong," she started, and fled up the stairs.

In the darkness of the bedroom, the sole illumination a feeble bluish glow from the Winnie-the-Pooh nightlight mixed with an amber dimness filtering up the stairs from the lighted rooms below, she gripped the railing of the crib, her chest tight and aching, finding, with her one free hand, the soft form that squalled and squirmed under the flannel blanket. Spurred by the rapid beating of her heart, her hand had caught the pace and slipped into an automatic pat-pat against the baby's warm back, a gesture, she realized, as necessary to console herself as the baby, who now breathed calmly beneath the steady rhythm of her palm. She kept up the patting until long after the breathing had grown quieter, more regular, then she clung for a moment to the edge of the crib, listening for the sounds coming from downstairs. A voice behind her startled her.

"Is Grandpa going to show slides?"

She whirled around so quickly that her son, sitting up in his bed, flinched as though she had struck him.

"Sssh!" she responded more fiercely than she had intended. Then, "Lie down. You'll wake up Angie," she whispered impatiently, pushing him back and pulling the covers up around him.

But he rose up again. "Is he? Can I go down and watch?"

"No. No. Nobody's showing any more pictures."

"But I heard—" He stopped and looked up at her in the dim light. "Honest? Not even Grandpa?"

She could hear the old man still rummaging around below. Mumbled words like "Jackson Hole" and "Jenny's Lake" drifted up the stairwell. "Well—maybe Grandpa, I don't know. But you've seen Grandpa's pictures before. You know what they are."

"I know—but I want to see them again."

Her foot brushed against something—the boy's trousers—crumpled on the floor beside the bed, and when she reached to pick them up, unidentified items dropped from the pockets and fell, jingling and clattering, to the floor.

"Now lie back down," she whispered irritatedly. "You've seen Grandpa's pictures lots of times." She glanced at the crib. "And if you whine until you wake up Angie, I'm going to be awfully cross."

"But just for a minute? *Please?*"

"*Steven,*" she said through her teeth. He lay back down against the pillow, and she knelt down to feel along the floor for the assorted rocks and spools and bits of wire that had spilled from the pockets.

"I really haven't seen them very much," she heard him say quietly. "Remember what happened that other time? Remember down in Coalville, at Uncle Keith J.'s? At Christmas—no, it was Thanksgiving. Remember when Grandpa brought his pictures? And then when he set them up after dinner, Uncle Keith J. and Daddy watched the ball game on TV, and you and Aunt Verda stayed in the kitchen doing dishes. We never got to see them. Grandpa and me waited, and then he finally folded up the screen and packed everything back up and went home."

"I don't remember that," she said, and the sound of her voice surprised her.

"Grandma said, 'I don't think anybody wants to see your slides,' and they packed it all up and went home. I never even got to see the bears."

"I think they went home because Grandma was sick or Grandpa had a cold or something. I can't remember." She stared for a moment into the dark, then picked up what items her fingers had found and laid them on the dresser, standing for some time before the darkened mirror.

"Please—can't I go down?"

She turned around and found him standing in his pajamas behind her.

"Oh, you make me so cross!"

He flinched again, but then said: "If you'll please let me go down, I promise I'll just stay five minutes," and he held up five fingers in the dim light.

She hesitated. "All right," she said finally and very quickly. "Be very quiet and get on your slippers and your bathrobe, and I'll let you go down this *one* time." She helped him into his bathrobe, pushed him toward the door, then turned back to the dresser before the darkened mirror, her fingers fumbling numbly with the odd shapes of his belongings she had gathered from the floor.

"Are you coming down too?"

She turned: "Sssh!" In the crib, the baby stirred.

His silhouette still hesitated in the doorway.

She motioned with her hand for him to go and heard his voice, small and innocent, say, "Don't you even want to see the pictures of you?"

Her desperate "Go!" was more nearly a cry than a whisper.

The baby raised its head from the blanket and cried out. She glared, her eyes blind with hot tears, at the now-empty doorway, then snatched up the baby in its blanket, and began pacing the darkness of the room.

"Close your eyes, close your eyes," she crooned over and over, her hand patting the quiet form in her arms more quickly, more forcefully, and much longer than was necessary. From downstairs she heard Grandpa: "Do you want to see some pictures of Yellowstone?"

"That's upside down, Grandpa," came Stevie's voice. Then: "Now it's sideways."

"Well, then, how about this one of your Mama by the old Chevvy?"

And she cried in the dark with only the little stream of colored light coming through the doorway from downstairs as the pictures changed.

Nazareno

The hot air was almost dizzyingly thick with the sweet, heavy, April smell of orange blossoms when Hulda Spencer got out near the cathedral in Seville and had to cling, for a moment, to the open door of the taxi to steady herself. In a whirl around her, horse-drawn carriages waited in the late afternoon shade of the rose-colored baroque buildings; tourists brandishing guidebooks, maps, and cameras shaded their eyes while they peered and pointed up at the Gothic spires and lacework overhead. The cab driver had already lifted out Hulda's two bags and stood snapping his gum and jingling some change in his pocket. She fumbled nervously in her purse for the money exchanged for her traveler's check at the airport; finding it, her fingers began to shake almost uncontrollably. The strange brown bills and silver coins felt odd and frighteningly unfamiliar in her hand. She examined each coin closely as she counted out the eighty-five pesetas registered on the meter, trying desperately to calculate the cost of this first daring expenditure and wishing her brother had been able to be there to guide her through these initial feeble steps.

Unsure of what might be customary, she chose not to tip him, yet she felt an immediate wave of guilt sweep over her as he took the money, gave an abrupt little snort, motioned his head toward an alleyway, then disappeared inside the taxi to roar it down the street and out of sight. It was strange: she had never ceased feeling uneasy as she had ridden through the smoky alien streets with the dark driver at the wheel, snapping his gum and watching her through the rear-view mirror. But now that he had left her on her own, with only a flick of his head to point out the narrow street she must take, she felt abandoned, doubly alone now, and almost wished she could call him back.

She was thankful that it was still light, though the watch hanging from a chain around her neck told her it was almost evening; and she was glad, too, that the streets seemed to be filled with other visitors, somewhat like herself. Yet she felt uneasy—first, because people just seemed to brush by without paying the slightest attention to her, and secondly, because when someone *did* look at her—two smartly dressed Spanish girls who stopped talking long enough to turn their heads in unison and stare at her before they went on chattering down the street—she was left feeling more uncomfortable than ever. Beginning to feel the weight of the suitcases, she almost stopped to rest in front of a travel agency; but then she caught her own reflection in the window and hurriedly moved on. Emma Lou and Wendell had written and advised her to travel light, but now she was beginning to think she had brought all the wrong things—her hemlines seemed wrong and her suit jacket suddenly felt big, and worst of all, she couldn't even think of anything in her suitcase she would rather change into. Two more Spanish girls clicked by on their platform heels, their long thick hair swinging back and forth as they walked, exposing smart gold rings against their smooth cheeks. Hulda caught herself turning around to look back at them, wondering about the tiny sweaters they wore over their blouses. Maybe it was the style, she thought, remembering how she had once given a perfectly good sweater to Deseret Industries when it had shrunk like that.

The noises around her made her uneasy: cars were honking and roaring down the narrow street behind her; from a balcony overhead a woman bellowed to some children running and squealing below; and from somewhere else a radio, at full volume, seemed to be grating out what she took to be the wail of a Spanish flamenco singer. And so she felt relieved when she finally found the sign pointing out "Barrio Santa Cruz" and, following the little street as it twisted back and forth, came at last to the doorway with the placard dangling overhead whose words she felt thankful to recognize: *Cama Y Comidas.* "It's right in the heart of the old section," Wendell had told her on the phone. She put down her bags in the cool entryway and rested before starting up the dark stairs, unsure whether to

50

feel exhilaration or terror at the prospect of the little adventure awaiting her.

She couldn't help feeling disappointed. It had been the thought of seeing Wendell rather than the Fair or Holy Week that had excited her, she was sure of that now; and, although he had tried to assure her over the phone at the airport that they would be getting together as soon as possible, it had not quite soothed her initial disappointment in not finding him waiting for her when the plane touched down in this strange and very foreign land so many miles from Fillmore, Utah. She wanted to pinch herself for being so selfish: she really *was* happy for their "news," and she couldn't wait to write Mama and Gloyd to tell them. And she *was* sorry that Emma Lou had been feeling so "under the weather," as Wendell had put it, and she understood—or at least she was *trying* to understand—what it must be like during those first few months of pregnancy. Yet the disappointment was still there, like a bruise inside her chest, and she couldn't forget it.

Standing there in the dim and unfamiliar hallway, smelling a musty mixture of damp tile and olive oil and hearing strange sounds from the street outside, she longed to be back in Fillmore, working at the public library or helping to put the supper on the table or doing something for Gloyd. The thought of Gloyd, most of all, caused a little twitch of pain in her chest. What would he be doing now? Leaving him had been the hardest part, and it almost made her want to cry remembering how he had looked with his face pressed against the glass at the Salt Lake airport, waving the little American flag with one hand and holding tight to the whirligig with the other. "Ever see a Mongolian idiot?" some crude man in a cowboy hat had whispered loudly to his sons as Mama had helped her push Gloyd's wheelchair through the crowd and up the little ramp to where they had to wait for the flight to be called. "He must be at least fifteen or sixteen years old," the man had said, and she had winced and tried to shut her ears, thinking of Gloyd's twenty-second birthday coming up in June.

She looked up the shadowy stairway now to what seemed to be a battered green door at the top. "Anyway," she could remember Wendell telling her over the phone, "I think you'll probably enjoy it a lot better there in town instead of being stuck out here at the air base all the time you're here. Especially with Emma Lou not feeling up to much." *But I could do things for her,* she had wanted to say—*help out around the house and fix your breakfast or whatever needs doing until she's on her feet again.* But he had sounded insistent, and the arrangements had already been made: two weeks' room and board all paid up, he had said, at a little place he had been able to find in the Barrio Santa Cruz, apologizing that it wasn't anything fancy but it was the best he could come up with at such late notice since most of the hotels and pensions in Seville had been booked for months before because of Holy Week and, the following week, the Fair.

She picked up her bags and started up the stairs toward the green door. A radio or television was playing loudly inside, and she had to knock three times before anyone came, and then, when the door finally opened, she was startled to see what seemed to be a dwarf standing before her. By the time she realized it was only a fat little girl with an enormous face staring at her from behind a pink lollipop, the child had called over her shoulder in an unbelievable operatic baritone—"Ma-maaa!"—summoning from the back of the house a disheveled middle-aged woman in a housecoat wiping her hands on a towel.

"*Que quiere?*"

Hulda felt her heart crowding into her throat as she tried to piece enough Spanish words together to make a coherent statement. "My brother?" she found herself saying. "*Hermano?*" She couldn't think of how to say *room,* but tried to point beyond the woman and the child to one of the doors behind them. The woman tossed her head to one side and cried out, "Pa-paaa!" The noise from the radio or television suddenly ceased, and an old man appeared in a doorway burping and fumbling with the top button on his pants. While the woman and the old man exchanged rapid comments Hulda could in no way understand, she tried to dig about in her purse for a letter with her brother's name and address on it, but this only puzzled them, and it was not until she tried again in Spanish, searched desperately for her passport, and then waited while the old man fumbled around in drawers and boxes until he came up with a note and a check in her brother's writing that they nodded and, with a string of "*Si, si, si, si*'s," took her bag and ushered her down a narrow little hall, the child with the big head, a toothless old lady, and a third lady from out of nowhere following curiously behind.

The room made her shrink even more inside her loose-fitting suit jacket, and her hands clenched, feeling terribly empty without the familiar handles of the bags they had taken from her. It was a tiny, odd-shaped room that was entered under the stairs but had a high ceiling with peeling plaster and what seemed to be a fifteen-watt globe dangling down several feet at the end of a multicolored cord. Though there were only three pieces of furniture, they managed to crowd the room: against one stained wall was a single bed, next to it a varnished nightstand with a vase of dusty plastic flowers, and towering over them both, between a yellowed wash basin and a green louvered window, was an enormous armoire with a huge key protruding from it and a full-length mirror reflecting cloudily and wobbily the bed and the plastic flowers. When they finally left her alone, she sat for a moment on the edge of the funny little bed, hugging her purse and rocking back and forth.

When the sounds from the street below startled her awake the next morning and she realized where she was, she saw the little streaks of sunlight trying to ooze through the louvered window across from her and somehow felt better about everything. She had had a hard time finding the bathroom the night before, and when at last the little girl with the big head had led her down the hall and around the corner to the tiny niche with the crooked door that wouldn't shut all the way, she had stood for a long time in the dark trying to remember why she had come to Spain at all. Earlier she had meant to freshen up a little and then maybe take a short walk back in the direction of the cathedral to see if it were lighted at night, but after she had written a TWA postcard to her mother and Gloyd and one to the ladies at the library, she felt so exhausted from the flight that she had just locked her door, pushing the little night-stand over in front of it, and then gone to bed.

But this morning things seemed better. She dressed quickly, had to wait for several minutes at the big oilcloth-covered table for a deep-fried piece of dough that sagged greasily on her plate and a cup of dark chocolate so thick that she left a third of it stuck in the bottom, then took her map and guidebook she had brought with her and went out into the morning-cool streets of Seville. She was astounded at how many women she saw shopping in house slippers and housecoats and how many Spaniards seemed to have blond or reddish hair. But what amazed her most of all was the way the men looked out of their shops at her and even stopped work to stare at her and call out little things that she couldn't understand. No one in Fillmore, she was sure, would ever believe it. Once she came upon a tiny little patio with a fountain where two children played with a kitten, and she wanted to kick herself for having finally decided to leave her box camera at home in Fillmore; what she *had* brought was some kind of camera that her cousin DeLyle had got overseas and was so complicated that, even though he had shown her how to use it after he had persuaded her to bring it, she had planned on having Wendell go over it with her a few times. Right now she could feel the camera's heaviness weighting down her purse, but she couldn't even remember how DeLyle had said to put the film in.

During the morning she peeked in several churches and saw, among the candles and the flowers, the statues of the Virgin being draped in jewels and velvet, in preparation for the coming procession. She even saw—much to her surprise, despite the pictures in her guidebook—two or three men on the streets who were already dressed in the robes and pointed hats that covered their faces except for the eyes and reminded her of pictures she had seen of the Ku-Klux-Klan. For a while she sat in a little park and practiced some phrases to herself out of her Spanish book; then, with the help of her map, she made her way back to the Barrio Santa Cruz, losing her way only two times, and rested in her room until the old man came and knocked and led her to the table with the oilcloth where she and some people who spoke only Spanish ate boiled potatoes and some strange fish.

She had hoped Wendell might have called and left a message, but when there was none, she decided to go out again for a little bit in the afternoon. But the names of the streets mixed her up, and she suddenly found herself by chance in the same quiet little patio where she had seen the children playing earlier. It was empty now and quieter still. From two to four-thirty, she remembered reading in the guidebook, was *siesta* time: the stores would be closed and the Spaniards were most likely taking a nap. She walked two or three times around the little patio, smelling the leaves and listening to the quiet dripping of the fountain, and decided at last she felt quite safe here and might as well just sit for a while on one of the benches in the shade and do a little more reading about what to expect during Holy Week.

She had hardly opened her book before something jarred the bench, and she looked up, startled, to see a man sitting down not more than a foot away from her. She tried not to look at him, making an effort instead to find her place on the page and focus on the words, but her hand suddenly began to shake so badly that she had to hold the book with both hands and pull it in close toward her chest, which seemed to be jolting now with every heartbeat. She didn't want to look around her or even look up at all, but the words on the page ricocheted without meaning against the throbbing walls of her mind while a faraway voice seemed to be screaming at her that she was a defenseless woman alone in a foreign country where a complete stranger had chosen to share her bench rather than any of the others—all of them empty—in this terribly secluded little patio. She felt she had to gather her things up and run immediately, but despite the almost electric humming in her head and the rapid jolt-ings of her heart, she found that she had no strength in her fingers or in her legs.

Above the high-pitched ringing in her ears, she suddenly realized that the figure beside her was also making sounds—hum-ming sounds—no, more than that, he was singing, actually singing aloud—although not too loud—the words of some Spanish song that made her back prickle and tingle, and she glanced quickly out of the corner of her eye to see that he had shifted his hands to his pockets and was now leaning his head back in order to stretch him-self out casually against the ornate bench.

Run for your life, Hulda Mae Spencer, a stern voice seemed to be trying to communicate to her over some faraway megaphone, and before she could decide whose voice it was—her mother's, Wen-dell's, Bishop LeFevre's, or simply some disguised version of her own—she was aware that the fellow had turned his head and that his eyes were on her.

"*Guapa,*" she heard him say. The word shot through her head, then lodged there, like a familiar box that you can't remember the contents of. *Oh my heavens*, she realized, *now he's actually talking to me*. She tried to get up enough strength to leap up from the bench and flee down one of the little streets.

"*Guapa*," he said again, and, although she couldn't be sure, it was almost as if he reached over and touched her shoulder or her arm.

She stiffened, prepared to leave, and shot him one last nervous glance.

"*Tu*," he said, and their eyes met. "*Tu eres muy guapa*."

She wanted to die. It sounded vaguely familiar to her, something she must have heard or read years ago in high-school Spanish, but she couldn't for the life of her think of what it meant, and she only knew it sounded obscene and that she had better ignore him totally and get out of there as fast as she could.

"Beau-tee-ful," he said, carefully, then flashed his even teeth in a smile. "You are beau-tee-ful." She really did want to die. And she knew why she had not leaped up the moment he sat down, even though she had only caught a glimpse of him: he was younger than she was, by at least ten years, she was sure of that, and fairly slender in build, but more than that, there was something about the nice black coat he had thrown over his shoulders like a cape or the way his dark hair curled against his ears as though he had just stepped from a shower that did not alarm her in quite the same way an older, bigger, sloppier person would have.

But she *was* alarmed: physically, she felt as if she would never be able to catch her breath, and mentally—well, she was sure she was on the verge of losing her mind, for no one had *ever* told her that she looked beautiful—except when she was nine years old and had played the rainbow in a Sunday School pageant.

He was looking at her now as if he had made a mistake. He tipped his head toward her, looking up at her from under dark brows. "American—you?" he asked, pointing a finger.

"*Si*," she found herself replying, though it sounded more like a question than an answer.

He seemed to relax immediately. "*Hablas español?*"

She was proud to have understood, but the question flustered her. "No," she said immediately, then: "I mean—well, *si*, a—a little. *Un poco*."

He asked her then something she couldn't follow at all, and before she could do anything but just flap her hands rather helplessly in her lap, he laughed and said, "I no can speak berry good the Eenglish. *Solamente un poco tambien*—just a leetle." He held his thumb and forefinger close together as if indicating a quarter of an inch. He was leaning in toward her now, and she could smell his shaving lotion and even a faint smell of potato chips on his breath. She leaned back but felt the wrought-iron arm of the bench pressing against her from behind.

"First time in *España*?" he was asking. "You like see *Semana Santa*?" *Holy Week*, she thought, but unsure of what his question implied, she only stuttered, and he went on, holding out his hand to her: "My name—Manolo." The way his lips and tongue said the name made her shiver. "Manolo Romero. And you?"

She thought of saying Mary or Carol or just not saying anything but leaping up and running across the patio, yet her voice, weak and shaky, was already telling him, "Hulda Spencer." He had her write it out on a piece of paper, then he tried it two or three times and said, nodding, "Berry beau-tee-full. New York City?"

For a long time they talked there in the shade of the trees while birds flittered about the fountain. Still uneasy, she nevertheless felt better when an old woman waddled into the patio leading a half-naked child and then sat crocheting on a bench across from them while the child chased the birds.

Manolo Romero, Hulda learned, was from Ronda, a place "berry berry beau-tee-ful" that one had to see in order to say he had ever been to Spain. What the boy did exactly was unclear to her, although he seemed to have had several offers to go to America or Canada and work. His father had some connection, also not quite clear to her, with Generalissimo Franco, and Manolo's mother's family had been extremely prominent in Granada and Cordoba— one or the other or both, she was not really sure. She was learning some new Spanish words, however, and she had him write them all down for her on the inside cover of her Seville guidebook. He was sitting very close to her now, and it made her shiver all over and wonder if the ladies at the library in Fillmore would ever believe her.

Finally he looked at his watch and, leaning his face closer to her than she could almost bear, he said, "Come, I show you *Sevilla y La*

Semana Santa." She had been preparing herself to say, "No, thank you," in case he offered to guide her around, but she remembered reading that the processions started about four-thirty and, not knowing where to find them and regretting that Wendell was not there to advise her, she gathered up her books and her purse, saying a quick little prayer to herself, and meekly followed Manolo out of the patio.

For most of the next hour, Hulda found herself lagging back while Manolo led the way through the narrow streets, pushed through the crowds that were gathering around the cathedral, and finally made arrangements to rent two little wooden chairs on a platform overlooking the street where hundreds of hooded penitents bearing crosses and giant lighted candles were already slowly filing. But she liked it when he tried to explain about the different fraternities making up the processions; about the elaborate lifelike statues of Christ and Mary accompanying each group; and the thirty-six squatty stevedores hidden by a hanging velvet drape, sweating and grunting underneath the weight of the ornate float supporting the sacred mannequins. Between his meager English and a few vague snatches of Spanish she recalled from her reading, she was able to feel at least a little more as though she were part of the celebration; otherwise, she thought to herself, she would have felt less easy watching the hooded men trailing by beneath their burdens—some choosing to carry as many as five heavy crosses at once—and hearing the uncomfortable funeral-like marches of the bands or the painful cry of a spectator leaning from a balcony to praise one of the Virgins in a short mournful song as her statue was carried by.

And so she really did feel a little better, she tried to tell herself, witnessing the long processions in the company of this young man rather than trying to fare for herself among the crowds—especially after it grew dark and the lighted candles and funeral music took on an even more eerie tone. And yet, she had never quite ceased shivering, and when he finally insisted she put his coat around her, the trembling became even worse. She didn't like how close he put his face when he talked to her, and when he turned once, smiling, and said, "Americans—much money, no?" it bothered her more than she could account for. But worst of all was when she could feel his eyes on her and she would hear him say, "Berry beau-tee-ful." It was a strange sensation, sending an icy shiver all the way down inside her at the same time that it made her stomach contract with a sharp little jerk. It wasn't true at all, she knew that, and she had long given up pretending that she would ever be anything but plain Hulda Spencer who worked at the library. And yet—there was one remote hope here somewhere: maybe there was something in the Spanish mind, something she didn't know about, something in their culture and their background, in their ideas of what was plain and dumpy and what was beautiful. She remembered the various men during the day who had called things to her and even made little kissing noises as she passed by: was it pure insolence or was it something else she didn't understand?

"You like something—for drink?"

"Oh, no, no," she said quickly. Then, looking at her watch and wondering if Wendell had been trying to reach her, she added: "I must go, I think."

"Go?" It seemed incomprehensible to him. "Why go?" he asked again, his hands and shoulders in a partial shrug. "We have some drink and *meriendas*—you know what is *meriendas?*—and then at ten o'clock maybe we eat some soup and the meat and the *tortilla española*. You know what is *tortilla?*"

It was all too difficult. She didn't know how to explain to him that she didn't drink alcohol, not even coffee or tea, and that she wasn't sure what a Spanish *tortilla* was and whether she would hate it, and that she wanted, more than anything right now, to be back in the place where she was staying, talking to her brother on the telephone.

But she went with him, through the squirming crowds, to a little place marked BAR where she hesitated outside until she saw several other couples standing up to the counter inside, drinking Coca Cola and eating little bits of cheese and shrimp and green olives on toothpicks. She nibbled uneasily at hers, had a few sips of carbonated orange in a glass that was wet and warm, and then told him nervously that she really had to go.

"What hotel?" he said, catching her by the arm outside the bar, and she realized that she was not quite sure she wanted him to know. His face, smelling of beer now, was inches away from hers, and he whispered huskily, "I come to your room." She pulled back, horrified, but he was still there pushing up against her in the crowd and gripping her elbow.

"You are berry beau-tee-ful. I love you."

She pulled away, wide-eyed, feeling the acid of the carbonated orange rising in her throat. "Hoolda!" she heard him call out, as she turned away from him, pushing through the hordes of people. And she ran terrified among the crowds until two policemen stopped her and, with the help of her map and her sobbed directions, escorted her back to the little pension in the Barrio Santa Cruz.

It rained almost steadily for the next ten days. The endless drip-drip on the other side of the intense green louvers became, for Hulda, a sort of clock, ticking away the days and the hours remaining of her stay in Spain. The rain came, at first, almost as a relief, sparing her from even wanting to step out into the streets and thus risking a chance encounter with Manolo Romero or, worse still, someone else like him; but when it scarcely let up during the rest of the week, she grew more and more listless, turning the pages of the books she had brought to read, and waiting for someone to come and tell her that Wendell was wanting her on the telephone.

Her little room in the Barrio Santa Cruz had seemed tiny enough at first, but now she had the impression that the rain was making the room shrink even smaller. The walls always smelled damp, and it seemed that whenever she turned around, the pink calcimine was rubbing off on her clothes and arms. Through the peeling walls she could always hear the TV screeching or booming in Spanish, and the little girl with the big head—Violetta, she was called—was either bouncing a ball against her door or standing there somewhere in the hallway, waiting to peek through the partially opened doorway whenever Hulda tried to go in or out. It was this, finally, that made her courageous enough to venture out, despite the drizzling rain and the chance that she might see Manolo Romero.

But the little excursions were discouraging too: on one soggy afternoon, she took her fold-up umbrella and wandered as far as the cathedral only to find out that all of the processions for that day were being cancelled because of the rain. On another day, when the rain seemed about to let up, she went even beyond the cathedral, passing by the police station where dozens of Americans shivered on the steps in the drizzle; a conversation in English, she thought, might lift her spirits, but when they told her how their cars had all been broken into and that there had been so many robberies during Holy Week that the police had almost started ignoring them, she came away feeling more depressed than ever. And the third time she ventured out into the rainy streets, just when it let up and looked as if the sky might clear, she started across a bridge and then noticed a man in a gray business suit, his newspaper tucked under his arm, urinating off the side of the bridge into the water, and she fled back to her pension so depressed that she didn't even feel like going out into the other room for dinner. There was something, however, that caught her eye just before she finally turned the corner in the Barrio Santa Cruz and started down the last little street. There, in a whitewashed alley, were three young Spanish boys pretending to be *nazarenos* in a shabby little procession. They carried crude crosses put together from broomsticks and scraps from a crate, and between the three of them, they supported on their shoulders a homemade float—a makeshift wooden platform on which some little girl's doll, with part of its hair missing and one eye closed, was swathed in a scrap of purple satin and surrounded by four squat burning candles. But the thing that really arrested her attention was the leader of the three: for although the two smaller boys couldn't have been more than eight or nine, the third one, who seemed to be giving directions, might have been as old as twelve or even fifteen: but he was Mongoloid, and the sight of him sent a wave of homesickness through her that made her almost fall back against the wall and stayed with her, even when she had practically forgotten the incident, for all the rest of the day.

But it was Wendell's calls that saved the week; and on Sunday, following his directions, she boarded the bus in the rain and rode out to the base where he took her to church and then brought her back to his cramped quarters where, together, they helped Emma Lou fix the dinner and then sat and talked while the rain poured down outside the window. It was quite nice being with them, she felt, yet a little dissatisfying too in its way, because Emma Lou seemed to mope around in her housecoat and was somewhat whiny and depressed, and Wendell, she felt, was trying almost too hard to make the afternoon comfortable and cheerful.

But even though the visit to the air base disappointed her, it was still a relief to finally be able to picture things the way they actually were—to know that she really wouldn't have been more comfortable out there with Wendell's wife in the condition she was in. She never had felt as close to Emma Lou as she had hoped, and now, she could see, was not the time to try to bridge the gap. Besides, seeing where they lived helped her to realize how crowded it would have been if she had been there all these days, sleeping on their couch and sharing their closet and their bathroom.

Still, she longed to spend as much time with Wendell as she could, and when he called her and said he had been able to get the afternoon off and was coming in to take her out, she was elated. He came in alone on the bus and, together, they went for a walk in the Maria Luisa Gardens. It was the first day of the *Feria*, the spring fair, and the rain stopped just long enough for them to hire a horse-drawn coach and costumed driver and be escorted beneath the dripping trees of the park where a few people were straggling about in flamenco attire. They stopped once and Wendell bought her ice cream, and for a moment it was almost the way she had pictured it from her home in Fillmore. She didn't tell him about her awful encounter with Manolo Romero, although she had thought she might; actually, she was still getting used to Wendell himself—how he seemed a little quieter, and had lost quite a bit of hair, and was shorter and stockier than she remembered. But when he finally said goodbye and took the bus back out to the base, she felt depressed and awfully lonely—for something, in fact, she couldn't even quite express.

The rain continued to drizzle on through the days of the *Feria*, and finally, with only two days of her vacation left, Hulda awoke feeling anxious and tense. Wendell had promised that nothing would stop him from being with her the last day of her vacation, and she was looking forward to that, but something still made her pace back and forth in her room while she listened to the rain dribbling against the green louvers. She tried to read for a while but her books didn't hold her interest. Hunger pains kept gnawing deep and low inside her, yet when she finally went out into the big room with the musty-smelling plants and the oilcloth-covered table, she could hardly bear to look at her food: soggy French fries lay drowning in a pool of dark tomato sauce; a few wilted shreds of lettuce floated in a plate of olive oil and vinegar; and her egg, when she touched it with her fork, seemed to quiver before it spread out in a bright burst of orange and ran stickily among the cold lumps of cauliflower.

She found herself hurrying inside the dark little cubicle where the toilet was, afraid she was going to throw up. It irritated her that the door was off its hinges at the top, leaving a gaping triangle above where anyone passing might peer in; and it bothered her that among the scraps of paper stuck on a nail inside the door were not only torn scraps of newspaper, but a chocolate bar wrapper, and even a large piece of wrapping paper from the bakery—*Pasteleria Salvador* imprinted in blue—with a daub of whipped cream still smeared on it. She felt on the verge of crying then, and when she flushed the toilet and the water spurted up over the edge and onto her shoes, she broke into tears.

If the sun had not come out shortly after two o'clock, she didn't know what she would have done; but as soon as she saw the little strips of bright light coming through the glistening louvers, she threw on her coat and almost fled out into the street. In her haste she had not even brought a book, but she resolved not to let that disturb her, hurrying instead toward the Murillo gardens nearby that she and Wendell had passed through twice on their outing a few days before. She found a place in the sun—a tiled bench near one of the gurgling fountains—and leaned her head back, closing her eyes, letting herself enjoy the way the warm sunlight felt against her cheeks and her neck. But every time she heard footsteps or the slightest sound of a voice, she sat up straight and opened her eyes; she didn't want to appear foolish, nor did she want to run the risk of missing anything. But there wasn't really much to miss: it was that sluggish *siesta* time, she remembered, and those who were strolling about among the flowers and the palms were more than likely tourists, though mostly Spanish, who had come into town for the *Feria* and, like her, were not about to stay indoors during this sudden burst of sunshine.

She watched two older women, one of them apparently deaf,

trying to carry on a conversation on the bench across from her. A child with a balloon ran into the tiny plaza and stuck his arm into the fountain up to his elbow until a guard came from somewhere, blowing a whistle, and chased him away. Next she watched two very young Spanish soldiers who took turns taking each other's picture, followed by a family with children dressed identically in matching sweaters and knee socks. The plaza had emptied and she had just leaned her head back to enjoy the sun again when a man's voice addressed her, startling her.

The sun was in her eyes at first, and she found herself clutching her purse and making ready to run before she realized that the figure looking over her like a big St. Bernard was speaking to her in English.

"I didn't mean to scare you, ma'am, but I was just wondering if you was an Amurican too."

He reminded her, in some ways, of a big cow. He was not exactly fat, just big, and his shoulders seemed to spill down in a heap from his almost neckless head. She wouldn't have thought to describe him as young—it appeared, in fact, that there was more hair on his arms than on his head—and yet the look on his face reminded her of one of the little schoolboys whom she would look up to see watching her as she worked at her desk in the library. He wore a short-sleeved shirt with sailboats and hula girls on it, and a camera, hanging from a strap around his neck, rested against his stomach. Before she could answer, he made a motion with his head as if asking permission to share her bench, and she immediately scooted to the far side away from him. She was relieved, however, that when he sat down, it was at the opposite end, and he seemed to perch rather cautiously and temporarily on the very edge.

"You are, aren't you—Amurican, I mean?"

"Yes," she replied quietly, giving the hem of her skirt two nervous little jerks.

"Me, too," he said, with a little laugh. "Where from?"

She told him.

"Me, I'm from pretty much all over," he went on. "Toledo, Kansas City, Des Moines, you name it." He licked at his lips and motioned toward some indefinite direction with his head. "Tell me, how do these people strike you?"

She glanced about her, unsure of what he meant. "Which—?"

"Any of 'em. The Spaniards. Don't they strike you as being awful high and mighty? I don't know about you, but I find these girls around here downright snooty. They prance around here with their noses stuck up in the air like they was God's gift to man."

Well, yes, she thought, she could see that. But the men—

"I mean," he went on, "I don't speak their language or nothing, but they could at least be civil. I'm not dirt, you know."

She felt uncomfortable and wished he would leave. And yet it did seem nice to talk to someone in English.

"You a schoolteacher or something?"

She told him what she did and that she had a brother nearby at the air force base.

His name, he went on to tell her, was Herb Gallacher or Gallegher or something like that, and he was a machinist. He had been in the navy (he showed her the tattoo hidden by the sleeve of his shirt) and had gone to technical school on the G.I. bill. He had come to Europe for three weeks with two other fellows from work, but they had decided at the last minute to rent a car in Amsterdam and drive to Hamburg, and he had heard about the festival in Seville and taken the train. "Gets awful lonely traveling by yourself," he said. "How about you?" She reminded him about her brother.

"Yeah, well, I'm glad I come, but I sure could of done without the rain. And some of this cockeyed snootiness." He rested back in the seat and stretched out his arm along the back of the bench. "There's some people you can talk to and some you can't."

That was true, she agreed.

She felt him looking at her. "You feel like walking around?" he asked. "We can just kick around the park here, if you want, or maybe mosey on over to the fairgrounds and see what's up. You can't get invited into any of those little parties going on over there unless you know somebody, but we can at least look around."

She hesitated.

"Feel like it?" he asked. "Or we can just walk around here, if you want."

It would be better than being by herself, she thought—especially when *siesta* time was over and the parks would start filling up with who knew what kind of people. "All right," she said, meekly. "For a little while then."

They walked for almost an hour, then he bought her an orange drink and some peanuts at a little stand, and they sat on a bench to watch an occasional costumed rider, with a girl in polka-dotted ruffles inevitably sitting side-saddle behind him, go through the park on his horse. Next they visited the Maria Luisa Gardens across the street, walking down the shady paths and investigating the various tiled fish ponds and statues tucked away among the greenery. She was embarrassed when he asked to take her picture by one of the fountains, but flattered nonetheless. Still, she tried to resist.

"I'd probably just break your camera," she protested. "Don't waste your film on *me*."

"Waste it? You're the best-looking thing I've seen since I left Des Moines, no lie, and I want to remember you for a long time."

She couldn't believe it. And it was going to be harder, she knew, for the ladies at the library in Fillmore to believe it.

"Let's put your coat over here on this bench and you can just lean up against that fountain there just like you belonged."

"Wouldn't you rather have those roses in the background?" she asked, but he was mainly interested in her, he told her.

She couldn't believe how many pictures he took. She had never had that many pictures taken of herself in her entire life, not even counting group pictures at family reunions or the time she and LaVee and Ardeen had spent the whole day at Otter Creek Reservoir. Some of the poses embarrassed her. He wouldn't let her just stand facing him: she had to turn sideways and look over one shoulder or sit with her back against a railing looking down at him out of the corner of her eyes. One shot of her poised on a wall particularly made her feel uncomfortable because her skirt kept creeping up, and every time she tried to pull it down he would yell at her to put her hands like this and then like that until she got so nervous that when he finally came over to arrange her himself and she smelled his after-shave lotion and the slightly sweaty smell where his shirt was damp under the arms, she started to shake until she almost fell off the wall.

After that he bought her some ice cream from a little cart on wheels, and while she sat on a bench licking the dripping vanilla from the stick, he excused himself and went off to visit the restroom facilities back in the trees. She had wanted to go too—for over an hour in fact—but just hadn't known quite how she was supposed to bring these things up. Now she sat uncomfortably on the bench wondering whether to wait or try to find the ladies' room while he was away. The problem was the camera: he had left her in charge of it and she hated to take it with her.

When she looked down at it on the bench, she could feel her face growing uncomfortably warm. She really hadn't done anything wrong, and yet she felt as if he had made her sit in positions and hold her shoulders in certain ways that weren't really her at all. In fact—she stared at the camera and wished she could destroy at least the *last* picture. She didn't want him to remember her like that. Don't ever open a camera with the film still in it, people had always warned her. The camera lay on the bench. What would happen if she opened it just a crack, she wondered. Would it ruin the whole roll or just the last two or three? She looked back through the bushes in the direction of the restrooms. Her heart pounded in her chest. It really did embarrass her, that picture; it really did. She swallowed and reached out one finger to touch the textured black finish and the silver chrome. She could open it very quickly, if she were only sure how. Glancing back once more to make sure he was not coming, she snatched up the camera, her hands shaking, and breathlessly felt for a clasp or button that would release the back. It was quite similar to the one DeLyle had loaned her, and the second she pressed her thumb upward against the side, the whole back of the camera suddenly snapped open. Holding her breath, she stared down at the instrument in her hands. The camera was completely empty.

She looked back in horror to see him coming through the trees. Quickly she snapped the back shut and dropped the camera on the bench; then she grabbed her purse and fled. She almost turned her ankle getting back onto the main path, and she could hear Herb calling after her as she ran. The horrifying thought that, in her panic, she might have started off in the wrong direction terrified her, but when she came to the edge of the park and stopped to catch her breath, she could see the children's playground of the Murillo

Gardens across the busy street and beyond that the old wall of the Alcazar and the Barrio Santa Cruz. The traffic light changed and she ran across the street, but as she looked behind her, there was Herb, camera in hand, running through the trees toward the intersection.

Through the Murillo Gardens she ran. A hot, tearing sensation spread across her chest, and her heart pounded in her throat and in her ears. Suddenly she saw the little alley leading to the Barrio Santa Cruz and she took it, still hearing Herb's voice calling after her. The streets, she thought in horror—she never remembered the streets; they all looked alike, and some of them seemed to go in circles and some were dead ends. Imagining she could hear his voice and even his footsteps behind her, she fled around a corner, seeing before her, at the end of the passageway, a blank white wall. "No!" she wanted to cry out; then catching an open doorway out of the corner of her eye, she ran into the safety of its shadows.

Something in the dark touched her arm and she gasped, unable to scream. It was a man. She shrank back against the doorway, wanting to die; and then she saw in the half-light that it was really the Mongoloid boy she had passed in the street a few days before. He reached out to touch her arm, patting her as if to calm her, and immediately, afraid her legs would buckle, she clutched him to her breast and held him there, nameless and locked within his own language, his stubby little hand still gently patting her, while she squeezed her eyes shut and released, at last, the inexpressible aching in her heart.

Serenade

He looked at himself in the bathroom mirror and felt immediately nauseated. "Delton," he started to address himself, but his voice came out hoarse and faint, and he had to clear his throat, and start over. "Delton Mecham," he tried, more bravely, "you're revolting."

He turned his head slowly from side to side, watching the effects of the overhead light on his pale forehead. At times the almost colorless strands of hair surviving on the shiny expanse of his head seemed to disappear in the glare of the light. "You're *twenty-eight*," he told his reflection, not certain how he expected it to react. "You're *twenty-eight years old*." Exactly what he meant by that he was unsure: twenty-eight seemed too old to be still unmarried; on the other hand, it seemed far too young to be so bald. He touched the tips of his trembling fingers to his cheek. "Fishbelly white," he heard himself whisper, staring incredulously at himself. He had had to reread the first few chapters of Huckleberry Finn just that day, and Twain's imagery suddenly seemed more appropriate for himself than even for Pap Finn. "You're fishbelly white." He remembered hearing an older girl in high school once say that someone she knew looked as if he had crawled out from under a rock. Could she have meant him? Had he always looked like that? He stared at himself. It was true: his skin had the unhealthy yellow-gray pallor that reminded him of the underside of a toad or of some grotesque and puffy thing that keels over on its back and kicks its tiny legs in the air when you expose it from under its rock.

He had felt uncomfortable in both of his classes all week. It had been as though the students were studying him, with frowns and a certain evident repugnance, through a pane of glass, like some freakish squid or rare and loathsome snake. It was a wonder to him now that they had not laughed. He flipped off the light switch and stood for a moment in the dark. Their comparing his meager abilities—to say nothing of his appearance—to Mrs. Quilter's graciousness and poise was inescapable, he realized that. But how could he bear to face them for the three remaining weeks? Three *days* had been painful enough. He wished that Mrs. Quilter had not had a nervous breakdown, and he wished that Dr. Munson had not asked him if he could take over for the rest of the semester. A month ago the prospects of being a graduate assistant and teaching two sections of freshman composition for the coming fall semester had seemed a stimulating, exhilarating challenge. Now the thought left him weak—like the thoughts of giving blood or letting Dr. Gottfredson grind on his teeth.

The day had been excruciating. For the rest of the world, he decided, it must have appeared to be a day of miracles, a day which, having been cleansed by the warm showers of the evening before, seemed to have risen fresh in a bath of pure sunlight to renounce once and for all the gray dreary winter it was leaving behind and to welcome a promising regeneration. The lawns, freshly green and yet unshaded by barely budding trees, had attracted hordes of students; ice cream cones dripped and peanut-butter-and-jelly sandwich crusts dried out while the students sprawled and laughed in the bright April sun.

But for him there had been no miracles, no hope, no promise. He had watched it all from the fifth floor of the Harold B. Lee Library while he had prepared a short lecture on Dryden, fumbled through the pages of *Paradise Lost*, and, time running short, hurriedly skimmed over once again Huck's first few adventures. Three times during the day, when it had been time to gather up his books and march across campus to his class, he had attempted to descend into that orgy of arms and legs sprawled upon the lawn—at least he had skirted it. But even keeping to his sidewalk and only nodding and feebly lifting his hand a time or two when he passed by someone he knew, he had felt out of place, overdressed, weighted and encumbered by the pull of his tie, the heavy wool of his coat, and the drag of his loaded briefcase.

Once or twice during the afternoon, while he had looked down from his library window, his imagination had leaped away from him, and he had almost pictured himself stepping back into a darkened alcove long enough to strip down to some daring costume—which, like Clark Kent, he would have hidden under his gray sport coat and trousers—and hurling himself, all muscles and bronze amidst envy and awe, down into that chaos of color tangled upon the new green grass. But he was far too much of a realist to allow such fancies much reign, and some thought always sent him shrinking back into his carrel and his books. Not even in imagination, he feared, did such a costume exist that could transform him into what he would really hope for; as far as dress was concerned, he had long ago realized that he was doomed. He had once been daring enough to spend a shameful amount of his savings on a wide-lapeled, flare-legged suit like those he had seen sported by his fellow schoolmates. But his courageous attempt to be part of the mod world had been disastrous: on the first nervous morning he had worn it, an acquaintance had stared at him and then, breaking into a shameless grin, asked him bluntly: "*Where* on earth did you dig *this* up?"

He drew closer to the mirror and examined the button-down collar of his shirt. It was beginning to fray. The thought increased his melancholy, for it was like an announcement that a close friend was moving away. Not that he had any really close friends—but he felt that he knew what it would be like. Actually, he had always found it difficult getting close to people. It was not that he was cold —or that he didn't try. He just didn't have the knack. Once he had admired a fellow he had met in a zoology class—a well-rounded, guitar-playing, sports-car enthusiast and track star—who, a year later, had lived on the same floor as he in Helaman Halls. After he had returned from his mission to Oklahoma and the other fellow was home from France, they had bumped into each other occasionally. He had always felt that part of the reason he felt close to this particular individual was that he knew—though he had long forgotten how—when his birthday was. This possession, like some personal secret discovered and guarded in silence, almost seemed to him to insure some intimate friendship. And once, when the time seemed right, he had mustered up—from where, he was later unable to imagine—enough courage to confide this fact to his "friend." In a moment of panic, suddenly not quite sure whether the date was October 30th or *31st*, he had decided to keep on the safe side and bumbled out: "Do you want to know something? I don't think there's been a year, when the end of October comes along, that I haven't thought of you."

The fellow had looked puzzled. "Why's that?"

He had swallowed and clung, for support, to his knowledge. "You know—your birthday."

The track star had looked even more surprised. "What do you mean? My birthday's in March."

He never saw him much after that.

He looked now at his collar and sighed. When this white shirt finally went, it would mean giving up the last link with his mission. His roommates four years ago had urged him to give them away to Deseret Industries, but what does one do with a limited budget and a drawer full of a half dozen or so perfectly good—or almost perfectly good—white shirts? He was not sure, not even now that this last one was going, that he would rush downtown and buy a red stripe like Scott's or a pink and purple print like Rick's, even though the teaching job would mean some unexpected money. He just wouldn't feel right in them.

He looked at his tie, and the old nausea surged through him. How would he ever get that spot off? Worse still, how had he ever been able to face his class? He had retied it so that the spot had been nearly hidden behind the place where his coat buttoned, but he noticed now how straggly and wrinkled it looked beneath the knot and he felt sick all over again. He had only had a few minutes, between his Neo-Classic exam and the second of his two English 101 classes, to find a corner in which to eat his Franco-American spaghetti. Long weary of bologna sandwiches, he had invested in a little thermos and sometimes took spaghetti or soup. But today had been a disaster. He had promised a student he would go over the comments with him that he had written on the boy's last theme (defending a *D* or an *E* grade was painful enough; why must he be obligated to justify an *A*–?), and finding vacant in A-203 JKB the desk he shared with three other graduate assistants, he had hurriedly gulped down his lunch in the three or four minutes before the boy arrived. The student had stayed for nearly half an hour, but it was what he had discovered just after the boy left that made him squirm now before the mirror. Feeling at least a modicum of victory in standing fast in his defense of the student's grade, he had happened to glance down, just as the boy left the room, and discovered in horror the big blot of tomato sauce and one cold string of spaghetti clinging to his tie.

His afternoon, precariously hanging together at best, had fallen apart. What could be done? Should he have called the student back and reprimanded him jokingly for not having brought to his attention the red blob decorating his chest? It was not his luck to manage situations like that with any degree of casual poise. Should he simply then have removed the tie and gone to class pretending nothing had happened? He would have felt naked and humiliated—as though the boy were passing notes around the room announcing why the tie was missing. So he had dabbed at the tie as best he could with water and a paper towel from the men's room and then retied it so that the now-glaring stain was hidden under his coat. But he had felt it shrieking at him all during that hot hour in the classroom when the hair had prickled on the back of his neck, and he had had the terrifying sensation that there was even spaghetti sauce still damp behind his ears and even dribbling down his forehead.

He sighed and heard himself make a little sound reminiscent of a wounded puppy. He looked at himself one last time, his eyebrows drooping as if they were about to slide down each side of his face. Was there any hope? He imagined he saw Dale Carnegie, Charles Atlas, and Norman Vincent Peale, come to collect their books, looking upon him now and shaking their heads with the same despair he saw reflected in the mirror.

Then Rick came home. He heard the bang of the door to their basement apartment almost at the same time that Rick, in cut-offs and a BYU T-shirt, barreled into the bathroom.

"Well, hello, gorgeous. Admiring yourself?" Rick stripped off the T-shirt and kicked off his tennis shoes. "What are you doing cooped up in this dark hole on a day like this? Afraid the light outside will spoil 'the light within'—like that El Greco dude?" Rick was in the shower running the water before Delton could get out an answer. He sighed once again and made a motion to leave; his roommate's muscular and suntanned form rotating behind the opaque glass made him envious.

"Hey—can I borrow your transistor again?" he heard him call out above the splatter of the water. "We're going up in the canyon. I'll be careful with it."

"Okay," he said, as he carefully shut the door and walked down the hall to the dark room with the bunk beds. "You're twenty-eight years old," he whispered to himself again. "You don't have a girl-friend"—he threw himself on the bottom bunk—"and you don't even have a tan."

He couldn't remember later if something he had dreamed had boosted his spirits or if it was just the fact that the long nap had the restorative effect of dissipating most of his depression, but when he awoke alone in the apartment about nine o'clock that evening and sat eating a Twinkie by the kitchen table, he decided that something had to be done. He was not sure where to start on the girlfriend problem; he had never dated at all in high school, had suffered through only three miserable blind dates throughout college, had been mercifully spared the problem during his mission, and then, while in the army, been frightened out of his wits by a buxomy woman with orange hair who had plopped down on the stool next to his and eaten the pickle off his plate while he had tried, terrified and aghast, to choke down the last bites of his pastrami sandwich.

No. He would not start there, just yet. He didn't have the knack. But he could do something about his appearance. At least it would be a start. He finished up his Twinkie and walked around the kitchen with a nervous determination. Tomorrow, he resolved, he would—no, not tomorrow, for tomorrow would be "Y-Day" and students would be up on the mountain whitewashing the block Y. But the next day, if the sun promised to shine, he would climb up to some secluded spot on the mountainside, his bathing trunks hidden underneath his clothes—again the old vision of Clark Kent's trans-formation glowed briefly in his mind—and lie in the sun until he began to resemble a normal human being.

He was out of school for three days the following week with the sunburn. He cried out whenever Rick and Scott put the cream on him, and when he was alone, he wept with pain. But the worst came when he started to peel. The lobster-red had turned a dull rose color, but as it came off in strips—from his back, his legs, and even from under the long mouse-colored hairs he combed in a special way to try to conceal his baldness—it left him looking for a time like some mythological relative, in various shades of pink, to a zebra.

But two things happened during this period. The first, and least significant, was his discovery of what seemed to constitute "the knack." He had been lying in his bed one night, uttering little "oohs" and "ouches" each time he shifted position and the sheet grazed his tender skin. Although the door was only open an inch or two, he was able to see the hallway to the small front room of their apartment, and at about ten-fifteen he heard the outside door open and watched Scott usher in some tall girl with long dark hair and a maroon pantsuit. Where they finally sat was out of his view, but he could not ignore, much as he tried, the sounds of Carly Simon, Elton John, and Blood, Sweat, and Tears that soon rocked forth from Rick's stereo and vibrated the print of *The Man in the Gold Helmet* on his wall. Nor was it easy trying to correct the stack of freshman themes left over from the week before while unable to avoid catching bursts of laughter, giggles, and assorted fragments of conversation:

"Oh, really—?" "—out of sight, man—" "Hey, that's swingin'!" He found himself counting the times he heard Scott say "really cool" (he lost track, however, and interest as well, after forty-seven) and Linda (was her name Linda? or was Linda the one before Michele threw him over?) tossed around "y'know" so much he hadn't even bothered to count. But sometime after midnight the stereo went off and no more records were put on. The conversation now drifted through the hallway and into his room almost without obstruction:

"—but why not? Haven't you prayed about it?"

"I *have.* I told you I have."

"Well, so have I—and I'm sure—in fact, I know beyond a shadow—"

"Please. Can't we just, you know, sort of—I mean, what's wrong with just going out—"

"Why don't we both pray—"

"Look. I've made a promise, y'know, and—"

"A promise not to pray?"

"Of course not, silly. Just wait—I mean, I've just got to wait until he at least, y'know, comes home. I just want to *see* him first—"

"But that's four more *months*—! Look: We've got something really cool going, right? You told *me* last night that—"

Delton was ready to get up and shut the door. He had been staring at the same misplaced semicolon for fifteen minutes. But his legs burned when he tried to move, and as he sucked in his breath to keep from crying out, he heard sounds of a different sort coming from the other room.

It was a hymn. Scott's voice, without accompaniment yet steady and clear, began to fill the quiet apartment and spill through the doorway:

> *Sweet hour of prayer,*
> *Sweet hour of prayer,*
> *That calls me from a world of care.*

Delton was shocked. He felt he had missed some transitional conversation, and the song struck him now as rather odd and out of place. Yet, after Scott had finished two verses and finally stopped, he thought he heard Linda sobbing quietly, and then, for the next hour until they finally passed within his view, their arms around each other as they left the apartment, he heard almost no sounds at all except an occasional sigh and what vaguely sounded like some muffled endearments.

He felt melancholy after they left and couldn't get his mind back to the stack of themes beside him. He feared he would be losing both roommates—Rick was already unofficially engaged—and the thoughts of living alone next year as he waded through stack after stack of freshman comma splices and dangling modifiers made him long for some nebulous feminine creature to listen to his *own* song, although he didn't have the slightest idea what that song was or would ever be.

At one-thirty in the morning, the themes untouched by his side, Delton was still sitting up in bed and staring at the wall when Rick burst into the room, bright-eyed and doing a little dance as he tossed off articles of clothing. "June 6th," he announced. "June 6th, babe, is going to be the big day."

Delton couldn't resist the question: "Rick," he tried, his voice a little hoarse. "Would you tell me something—something personal?"

Rick stopped, his fingers in the air, in the middle of some step borrowed from *Zorba the Greek*. "Well—that depends—" The look he gave Delton made him feel he had overstepped his bounds.

He got it out as fast as he could: "What I mean is, did you ever sing to Cheryl? *Hymns*, that is?"

"Hymns?" He looked puzzled. "Boy, you *are* getting personal!" he chided. Then he broke into a grin. "Sure—once a few months ago when we were parked up by the temple. That always gets them."

He didn't feel that he dare ask anything more, but his mind immediately became a vast darkened parking lot in which earnest young men, each warbling his own hymn to his own girlfriend in the dim privacy of his own car, became a part of a gigantic chaotic chorus performing nightly at the mouth of Rock Canyon. And after the bedroom light was finally turned off and he had tossed for an hour or more, it was this cacophonous choir that eventually sang him to sleep.

The second event that happened during this period was clearly the more momentous of the two: at the beginning of spring term, he met Lois. She was tiny and fragile, with pale skin, a slightly pointed nose, and a frail little voice; but within a week after he met her working in the reserve room of the library, he was certain she was the love of his life.

It was already May, and in the evening the smell of the lilacs made him dizzy. He found himself taking nervous walks around the block in the fresh night air—not the desperate melancholy walks he had taken earlier while the ground had been frozen in muddy ridges and patches of snow had crunched crustily under his feet—but walks that sent him striding, almost leaping, excitedly down the sidewalk, checking his watch at every streetlight until ten-thirty arrived, and then racing up the hill and across the quad to the library, his determination to be on time always assuring his arrival at least twenty-five minutes before the reserve room closed.

He was not entirely certain that *she* was certain he was the love of *her* life, however. She had not openly demonstrated any overwhelming warmth—something which, he concluded, probably prevented his fleeing in terror from the whole idea—yet she was decidedly civil and had never, as he recalled, betrayed any sign of being about to burst into laughter whenever he appeared, his face still mottled in various shades of pink from his Y-Mountain episode. In fact, he often thought to himself, elatedly, "If she likes me now—just wait until I've *completely peeled!*" And when, after nearly a week of walking her home, stopping once for onion rings and once for root beer floats, she asked him to reserve a date for dinner at her apartment, he felt quite sure that the world was becoming for him a rather different and marvelous sort of place.

Because the date set for the dinner was a whole week away, he anxiously began making plans for the weekend at hand. He found, however, that she was going home (to Afton, Wyoming) and would not be back until late Sunday night. The weekend was devastating. Friday night he loitered around the library just to be near the place that reminded him of her, but the couples flocking to the Varsity Theater and walking arm-in-arm across the moonlit campus depressed him. And on Saturday night he wandered through the streets downtown; but here again the couples, hugging and laughing as they waited in lines in front of the Academy, the Uintah, and the Paramount, made him melancholy and impatient for his love's return.

On Sunday evening, he walked by her house every half hour until, from where he stood in the shadows of the trees across the street, he saw a car drive up and watched as someone let her out and removed her suitcase from the trunk. In order not to seem too eager, he paced back and forth under the trees for ten more minutes, then rushed to her door and, after some time, convinced her to go out for a little walk while the weather was so nice. All weekend he had held imaginary conversations with her, yet he had difficulty now remembering even one of the polished and eloquent things he had imagined saying. Earlier in the weekend he had even thought of preparing a long letter that he could leave with her roommates or slide under the door, since a written explanation of all that was presently churning inside him would have allowed him to select just the right words and arrange them in just the right way. The idea had been dismissed, however, when he recalled what had always seemed to be his fate: he always managed to inadvertently bumble up the key words. Once, when he had entered a short story contest in junior high, his disappointment at not having placed at all (out of only five entries) had been embarrassingly magnified when he discovered, on the final page of his rejected entry, a glaring typographical error in the last sentence: ". . . and he lay there on the cement, his heart thorbbing."

And so, as they walked slowly up the hill in the dark, beyond the lights of Heritage Halls, then Deseret Towers, and finally Wymount Village, he fumbled for the proper words to explain the emptiness he had felt in her absence:

"How was the weather in Afton, Wyoming?" he managed.

"Just fine."

"Oh. Well, I guess it wasn't so bad here either," he found himself saying. "Anyway it didn't rain or snow or anything like that."

And on they walked, mostly in silence, up the road to where the golden spire rose out of the white temple, luminous against the night sky. Four or five cars had pulled off the road. From one he thought he heard a squeal, and then a high-pitched voice shrieked, "It's absolutely fantastic! How on earth did you ever find out my ring size?"

Lois snickered, and Delton reached out impulsively in the dark for her hand. He caught her shoulder bag instead, and not knowing what to do, clung to it. They were both out of breath from the long climb up the hill, and he stopped now to lean back against the wall surrounding the temple, panting in the darkness and still clinging to the strap of her purse.

His heart was pounding. He felt his free hand move almost instinctively to his mouth, but he resisted the urge and left it clenched stiffly by his side: he had already bitten his fingernails down to the quick while pacing under the trees waiting for her return. Once he had started saving the little half-moon-shaped slivers that would fall on his books and papers as he gnawed away at first one hand and then the other while he studied. He had kept them all in a little envelope. But then it occurred to him that if he could remember to save the nail-bitings, then he could remember not to bite them at all. So he had thrown the envelope away and gone on nibbling unconsciously at various moments of the day. He had wished since that he had kept his little collection; it had made quite a little lump in the envelope. Besides, what else did he have as a monument to his suffering?

The pounding in his chest seemed to have risen to his throat, and he found himself swallowing over and over to hold it back. His hand, still attached to her shoulder strap, suddenly started to quiver. He clutched tighter. Lighted by the moonlight as well as the glow from the temple, her long hair excited him. He was almost close enough to it to get a faint shampoo smell. He swallowed. He had never been this close to a girl before. He knew that he had to do something. He couldn't just go on sniffing her hair and gripping the vibrating strap. A hymn, he thought anxiously. What hymn? He tried frantically to concentrate, but the only things that would come to his mind were "When We're Helping, We're Happy" and "Give, Said the Little Stream."

At that moment, he imagined he felt her pulling away from him, and in desperation he grasped at whatever words offered themselves. He almost jumped when the sound of his own voice cut through the darkness:

The spirit of God like a fire is burning . . .

He detected a warble, a sort of unintended vibrato that unnerved him; but he tried to make up for the unsteadiness of his voice by an increase in volume that surprised even himself. He went on with the verse and into the chorus—

We'll sing and we'll shout
With the armies of heaven,
Hosanna, Hosanna, to God and the Lamb!

—hoping that the tune was close enough. It sounded right to him, but he had been told before—usually by frowns, but once verbally and explicitly by an acquaintance—that he had a tendency to stray somewhat from the actual melody. Caught up in the fiery momentum of the hymn, he almost decided to go on with all four verses, but something in her look—something akin to awe—finally made him stop after the last line of the chorus.

For him it was a triumph. He wasn't sure what to make of the little patter of applause that came from one of the nearby parked cars after he'd finished, or the fact that someone had rolled down a car window and shouted "Encore!" but whatever uneasiness accompanied him as they walked back down the hill in the dark was overridden by an almost thrilling sense of accomplishment. The air tingled on the back of his neck and his clothes felt damp, but for him it had been a demonstration of almost unprecedented bravery.

Serenade

Neither of them said much on the way home. But he felt that her remark—"Do you—uh—sing very much?"—was not without some warmth, and at least demonstrated an interest in his daring performance on the hillside. And he hoped that the sense of triumph running through him was warranted—that he had not only become victor over his own trembling self, but had conquered as well the fearful territory that had separated him and the love of his life. Not daring to risk what was beginning to seem an auspicious advance in the right direction, he refrained from kissing her goodnight when they reached her porch. Ahead of him glowed the Saturday dinner date, and he determined that, by then, he would be prepared for anything.

He was not, however, prepared for what happened. It turned out to be an unsettling week; with final exams looming ahead, he found himself buried in note cards and rough drafts of papers he had to complete for his own graduate classes, and inundated at the same time with the fresh deluge of freshman research papers, most of them either plagiarized or just honestly badly written. He tried to allow time to be at the reserve room of the library, but the room was overrun now with the semester's procrastinators, and he could barely see Lois over the heads of the students that flocked to the counter with their book requests scrawled on tiny white slips. After work she begged to flee home to study for her own exams, and he was left to go back to his dreaded note cards and rough drafts and research papers. The only near-bright spot in the week happened one evening when he was buying Twinkies at Carson's Market: waiting at the checkstand, he heard someone call out his name and looked up to see a large freckled girl waving a chubby hand and standing in line at another cash register. "I hear you're coming to dinner Saturday," she said, and, evidently noticing the startled look on his face, added quickly, "I'm Phylma—remember? One of Lois's roommates?" He felt embarrassed as he left the store that he hadn't remembered her at first, yet this feeling was gradually replaced by one of elation when it occurred to him suddenly that the anticipation at Lois's apartment somehow miraculously rivaled his own.

By Friday night his excitement for the following evening was so strong that he could hardly contain himself; but he finally resisted all temptations to make his usual nightly pilgrimage to the campus at ten-thirty, and restricted himself, instead, to the narrow asceticism of the kitchen table, assiduously filling the margins of the students' papers like a monk illuminating ancient manuscripts. And on Saturday morning, he burst out of his basement cloister to regain contact with the world, getting first a haircut, next buying some new after-shave lotion (although if Hai Karate really accomplished what the advertisements promised, he determined to use it sparingly), and finally splurging at The Emporium on a gift-wrapped box of chocolate-covered raisins.

But he was not prepared for what happened. Even when he stood ringing the bell in the shadows of the porch and a massive silhouette loomed up against the drawn shade of the front room window, even when Phylma opened the door in her turquoise taffeta dress and he saw the tiny rhinestone earrings clinging to her ample lobes and the matching necklace lying on her moist and freckled neck, he failed to realize what had taken place. As she ushered him in, Phylma smiled a self-pleased smile, like a little girl who knows she has done something special, and he caught a glimpse, beyond her towering figure, of a small table—complete with a long white tablecloth, a bowl of orange flowers, and matching ostentatious candlesticks—set, very meticulously, just for two. She plopped herself down on the creaking sofa and patted heartily the cushion next to her for him to sit down. He did.

"Now," she announced, and held up one fat palm as if to prevent him from suddenly fleeing, "everything is almost all ready." He felt the prickles on the back of his neck—the old spaghetti sauce dripping down behind his ears and under his collar. He saw the tip of her pink tongue peek out quickly and dart along the edge of her lipsticked lips; her eyes had the sparkle of a child about to pull a Halloween prank. "There's been one teensy-weensy change," she began. "Something came up and Lois had to go home. To Afton, that is. She had this ride, you see, and she meant to call you, but, anyway, she didn't and she asked me to, and I guess I should have, but anyway, I ended up not calling either. The stuff was all bought and in the fridge so I just figured, what the heck, with you already planning and all, why not just go ahead and enjoy ourselves? I probably would've been the one that had to cook it *anyway*." She hesitated a moment, as if for his approval; and then, as if fearing she might not get it, she leaped up and put a record on the phonograph. He was still stunned, but he recognized the music as the overture to some opera.

Towering above him in her rhinestones and turquoise taffeta, she reached down one shapeless hand, the fingers like pale and puffy sausages, offering to help him up. "Should we?" she asked with a bounce in her voice. For a moment he feared she was asking him to dance around the room with her, but then decided she was taking him toward the table with its carefully folded napkins and shiny goblets. He imagined the warm spaghetti sauce dripping down his icy neck again, and he almost collapsed at the table.

"Could I—uh—wash my hands first?" he managed to ask, hoarsely, as she pulled out a chair for him to sit on. She beamed and led him through a doorway to a darkened hall. But as she pushed ahead of him and moved through the partially opened door he became terror-stricken: he had a frightening vision of her accompanying him to the sink and, like some robust and helmeted Athena out of a painting by Rubens, taking charge of the situation —running the water, lathering him amply with soap, then drying him lustily with some mammoth fuzzy towel. Instead, however, she flipped on the light and immediately swept down with a swishing flourish a blur of nylons and other things he tried not to see that had been hanging on the shower-curtain rod. She beamed at him, a perceptible pinkness momentarily obscuring her freckles, and then she swooped past him, leaving him leaning against the sink, stunned and drained by the events of the past few minutes, and unable to blink away the fluorescent image of her lingerie.

The whole thing was a joke. He still felt limp and partially numb, but he began to sense that the surrealistic shock of Lois's absence and Phylma's towering presence was wearing off, and he was about to see clearly what had taken place. He was the victim of some mean joke. He gripped the basin and closed his eyes to shut out the thought. They had played a trick on him. "How can I get out of it?" he imagined Lois wailing, and then he pictured her eyes widening as she said, "I know! I just won't be here and you can dress up in—" It was true. The evening was too grotesque, too bizarre, to be anything but a joke. Perhaps Lois had been in the bedroom watching everything through a crack in the door. He imagined Lois and Phylma both even now, their hands clasped over their mouths to stifle guffaws, retching with laughter in the hall. He felt dizzy and noticed that he still clutched in one hand the box of chocolate-covered raisins tied with a gigantic pink bow. He felt humiliated and he looked for someplace to discard it. He finally propped it up on the back of the toilet between the Noxema and the Clearasil.

He was still weak when he left the bathroom and stepped out into the darkened hall. He had taken a deep breath before opening the door and had decided to announce quite bravely that he could not stay. But he hesitated when he saw the darkness of the front room. Not only had his foot become entangled in the telephone cord, but he also fancied for a moment that the lights might suddenly flash on and Lois would shout "Surprise!" and the nightmare would be over. It was not, however, as dark as it had seemed to him at first. The candles had been lit, and Phylma and her rhinestones glittered in the flickering light. He could smell incense burning, and a gypsy violin whimpered from the phonograph.

Before he could react, she had swept a chair under him, shaken out his napkin, and was ladling steaming onion soup, complete with croutons and shredded cheese, into his bowl. He ate as if in a trance, listening at any opportunity for some sign that Lois was hiding in the bedroom. Phylma herself ate heartily—two helpings of soup, ample portions of what she announced was *champignons au gratin* and *coq au vin*, and an unaccountable number of twisted, sugared breadsticks—but she never once allowed the conversation to lag: she talked of Goshen, of her family (nine brothers and sisters), of how she wanted to be a nurse, then an opera singer, and finally just a first-rate wife and mother, of her interest in Rudolph Nureyev and volleyball, of her collection of salt and pepper shakers, of her longing to visit Venice, Italy, and Gallup, New Mexico. But she showed an equal interest in him: what foods did he like, what did he think of Maria Callas, had he ever had a longing to teach school in Pago Pago?—and dozens of other questions. Finally, as they were eating *pot chocolat au creme*, she dabbed quickly at her mouth with her napkin, swooped off to find her *Treasures of Truth* albums which she showed him at the table, and then ushered him over to the piano where she seated herself and announced, "Lois tells me you like to sing."

Serenade

He had never regained his strength from the time he had stood on the porch ringing the doorbell almost two hours earlier, and now he felt all of the blood draining from his head. The spaghetti sauce again. But Phylma saved the moment by sweeping across the keys with a music-hall flourish and, in a startling tremulous contralto, breaking into the "Habañera" from *Carmen*. He quickly took the opportunity to sit down on the sofa nearby—partly because his legs seemed rubberized, but also because it offered him the role of spectator rather than performer. He felt it his duty to look at her from time to time while she sang, but whenever his eyes met hers with her pale eyelashes surrounded by ample lavender eye shadow, he felt his own eyes twitch away and seek out the cording along the edge of the couch or the tassels on the corners of the satin pillow he found scrunched up in his hands. But when it occurred to him that her voice was dissolving into a whistle, he was compelled to focus his attention on her. It was true. She was whistling. It was a whistle unlike anything he had ever heard. While her shapeless fingers trilled and rolled a grand accompaniment up and down the keys, she whistled the melodies of one tune after another in a low, bird-like warble that reminded him of water filling up a plastic dishpan.

It was impossible now to look at her, but he was not sure how long he could go on staring at the pillow in his hand. He finally let his eyes steal a quick glance at the swaying figure looming over the piano by his side. Under pale brows squirming with expression, the lavender eyelids were closed on the large upward-tilted face as her head rocked dreamily back and forth in time to the music. From her puffing freckled cheeks and the mouth shaped into a tiny O came the whistled strains of the theme from *Romeo and Juliet*.

He swallowed nervously. It was a joke after all; it had to be. He stared earnestly at the pillow for confirmation. But suddenly the song had ended, and he felt one of her hands slip from the keyboard and fall lightly on his knee. His glance ricocheted from the pillow to her face, but his stare remained the same. She had removed her hand now and had folded both of her hands across the top of the small piano, her face coming forward to rest on them just a matter of inches away from his own twitching face.

"Delton," she began, her voice frighteningly soft. "I've never said this before to a boy in all my life." He felt his back go suddenly

85

very straight, and he was certain now that the spaghetti sauce was streaming coldly down his spine.

"I feel very oddly moved," she went on, and he thought he saw her chin quiver slightly before his eyes switched back to the pillow. "What I mean is—well—I feel that our—uh—getting together to-night was—somehow—*meant* to be."

He could feel no strength at all in his body. Something ran through his veins that made him feel he was being embalmed.

"I mean—" she went on, "God *does* move in mysterious ways."

His own moving was a mystery to him, for the next thing he knew he found himself back in the bathroom leaning against the door, his chest heaving rapidly as though he had run there from a great distance. He could not remember what he had said to excuse himself or how much more she had said, but his mind raced now and his temples throbbed as he tried to think of what must be said when he finally had to go back through that door. His eyes sought the tile walls pressing in on him, but they found no window. Instead they rested on the box tied with the pink bow. Maybe he could give her the box of chocolate-covered raisins and leave. It had not been a joke. It had never been a joke, and now it was certainly not a joke. He almost pitched forward and fell against the sink. Gripping it with both hands, he glared at himself in the mirror. "Delton," he whispered with a hoarse earnestness, "what are you going to do?" He waited for the reflection to answer; but it only stared back at him with a new terror of its own.

·

Bus Ride

By the time Mrs. Winterrose and the lady from Fredonia boarded the bus at Kanab, there was really only one good seat left. Not that all of them were taken—there was one near the front by a snoring Indian, another further back by a fat lady whose arm seemed to overflow into the vacant seat, and one by a sleeping soldier, his tie loosened and coat folded across his lap, his thick short hair making a greasy smudge against the window. There were quite possibly others in the back of the bus, but even before she was halfway down the aisle, Mrs. Winterrose was sure she detected a smell of alcohol, and this, along with the glimpse of an unshaven fellow in a denim jacket scuffling with two giggling girls near the back, settled the question of venturing any further toward the rear.

The good seat was midway down the aisle, the one next to it occupied by a harmless little mouse of a girl with glasses and frizzy hair the color of rust. A copy of *Screen Stars* with Jacqueline Kennedy Onassis on the cover was spread face down across her knees, and Mrs. Winterrose quickly tallied the advantages and disadvantages of this vacant seat and decided to take it. It was usually always good to sit beside someone who read because they were not quite as apt to ramble on and on about themselves and things nobody else cared about, and what they did say was liable to be somewhat sensible. Once she had been stuck by a woman from Annabella who, all the way from Richfield to Salt Lake, had described in detail every operation and personal disorder she had had in her life and who had made Mrs. Winterrose so nauseated she had had to put away her bacon and tomato sandwich half eaten and ride all the rest of the way to Salt Lake fearing every minute she was going to have to ask the bus driver to stop for her. Another asset, according to Mrs. Winterrose's practiced tally, was the very nature of the reading material, since Mrs. Winterrose herself was from "Utah's Little Hollywood," as the *Salt Lake Tribune* had once called Kanab, and it was always nice to sit by someone who appreciated the fact. Equally important in her decision, however, was simply the girl's appearance. Definitely not what you would ever call a raving beauty, Mrs. Winterrose agreed with herself, but then not one of your hard, gum-chewing girls with the painted eyes either who can't stop twisting around in their seats to see what the boy three rows behind them is up to. Some pathetic disparity in the girl's washed-out, peaked face and Jackie Kennedy's self-assured smile touched Mrs. Winterrose's understanding spirit (Zelda Barnhurst had told her right to her face that she didn't know of a living soul who saw through things quite so clearly as Mrs. Winterrose), and she determined then and there to invite herself to the seat by the window and see if she couldn't do something to bring a little cheer and perhaps even a spark of hope into the life of the pale little thing with the unfortunate permanent.

The lady from Fredonia was still huffing down the aisle, maneuvering two overflowing plastic bags in front of her and dragging another one behind, and Mrs. Winterrose felt it her duty to turn back for a second to make sure she had at least got on. After all, they *had* suffered the twenty-two-minute wait for the delayed bus together. Fellow sufferers or not, however, Mrs. Winterrose did not feel obligated to be linked forever with the lady from Fredonia since they had not even introduced themselves—despite the fact that the lady had told her all about her son's job with Thiokol and the suitcase that the bus line had ruined for her once when she went to visit her daughter in Tacoma. Mrs. Winterrose looked back, smiled as sociably as she could, and then, feeling compelled to assume a duty-doling role, gave her head a little jerk in the direction of the soldier, as if to say, "You cheer up the one in uniform while I handle this wallflower back here with the problem hair." The lady from Fredonia evidently got the signal, for, although Mrs. Winterrose thought she detected a little disappointment in the woman's puzzled look, she saw her hoist her three billowing bags one by one up into the rack above the seats, poke at them two or three times to make sure they were secure, then, giving the back of her crepe dress a little yank and looking around to see if anyone noticed, plop herself down into the seat beside the sleeping soldier with the greasy window.

Mrs. Winterrose eased herself discreetly into the seat by the girl with the washed-out face, who had gone back to reading her magazine. She wasn't surprised that the girl didn't acknowledge her; Mrs. Winterrose knew shy types just as well as all the other types she had encountered in her long years of service to church and community. Yet, she had the odd sensation that, whenever she was not looking at the girl, the girl was looking at her; but every time she turned her head quickly to catch the girl's gaze, she always found her even more engrossed in whatever she was reading. Once Mrs. Winterrose strained her neck a little to catch the title of the article, but the girl just turned the page and went on reading.

When the driver got in and started up the engine, and the bus pulled away from the Trail's End Cafe and started off into the night, Mrs. Winterrose shifted to make herself comfortable and decided it was time to break the ice. "How far north are you going?"

The girl glared incredulously at Mrs. Winterrose without lowering her magazine, looked back as if to check what page she had been on, then laid it on her lap and said, "Alaska—eventually."

Mrs. Winterrose was not sure she had heard right. She had fully expected to hear Salt Lake City. "Oh," she said, then decided she had better make sure she had not misunderstood. Once she had sat by a young college student and asked him his major twice and not been able to catch it either time. She had spent the whole trip thinking up sensible questions to ask about it that might lead her to discover what the word was that she had missed without giving herself away (and thus appearing to have a serious hearing problem, which she definitely did *not* have) but they had finally reached Salt Lake and she had said good-bye to the boy without ever finding out what it was.

"Did you say—Alaska?"

"At least. Maybe the Yukon. Anywhere as long as it's as far away from here as I can get."

"From Kanab?" asked Mrs. Winterrose, noticing an incredulity in her own voice.

The girl glared at her as though *she* were not hearing right this time. Then: "No. From Arizona. From the U.S. if I can help it. From the whole rotten schtick."

Mrs. Winterrose wondered if maybe *she* should have sat by the soldier and let the lady from Fredonia cope with the wallflower's problems. She rearranged her purse on her knees and then tried once more.

"To feel that way, you *must* have had something disappoint you—"

"Some *thing?*" the girl asked loudly, and Mrs. Winterrose shifted uncomfortably, afraid people would look back to see if the girl were being molested. "What, for crying out loud, *isn't* disappointing?"

I knew it, Mrs. Winterrose told herself. If the girl's shyness was not quite what her appearance tricked you to believe, there could at least be no mistake about her problem, Mrs. Winterrose was sure of that.

"Well, there's bound to be a few ups and downs," Mrs. Winterrose agreed, "but I can tell you one thing; there's an awful lot of girls in this world who think there's nothing more important than having a dozen boyfriends and going to every party, dance, and dog fight in town, and who are going to be in for a big surprise once they get married and find out—"

"Marriage," the girl broke in, "is just a big bunch of bull anyway."

Mrs. Winterrose felt as if someone had thrown a pitcher of ice water in her face. Now she knew she was hearing right, but wished she were not.

"It's on its last leg, let's face it. The whole institution'll be dead in a matter of years. That's why I'd never think of marrying this kid I've been living with even if he wanted to—which he doesn't."

Mrs. Winterrose felt the warmth of the bus close in upon her; she could find no words, could scarcely, in fact, find her breath. The girl evidently did not need her services—at least not the ones she was prepared to offer.

"Anyway," the girl went on, picking up her magazine again, "he's into this thing in Canada, something he really grooves on, and I might join him and I might not. The guy I lived with in Taos before that is out of the pen for pushing hash, and he's supposed to be hitching his way up to Fairbanks right now, so I'm gonna meet him there."

Mrs. Winterrose pulled herself together and sat without saying a word for several seconds. Then she decided to try a new approach.

"I see you're reading *Screen Stars*." If she worked up to it right, it would only be a matter of minutes before the girl's eyes would be bugging out as she told her about how she had been an extra in *Thunderhead* and *Bob, Son of Battle* and how she had met Preston Foster face-to-face in front of Bradshaw Auto Parts.

But the girl just glared at her. Mrs. Winterrose stole a glance at the page the magazine was opened to, caught a glimpse of Barbra Streisand, and whispered, confidingly, "It's fun to read about them, isn't it?"

The girl continued to look at her. "It's the biggest bunch of barf I've ever read," she said flatly. "Somebody must've copped this and then ditched it in the ladies john in Phoenix. I should've left it there where it might've been of some earthly use." Before Mrs. Winterrose could gather her wits to think of what to say, the girl had gone back to her reading.

Mrs. Winterrose stared out into the dark, uncomfortably aware of the heat now. She wanted to turn to someone and say, "It just doesn't let up, does it?" but she noticed that the lady across the aisle —a thin woman whose sagging face gave the appearance it was on the verge of slipping down into a wrinkled heap around her neck— was bundled up in a coat with a diseased fur collar. Well, she said to herself, it takes all kinds to make a world. She rummaged in her purse, came across a program from Jasper Showalter's funeral and fanned herself with it. She surveyed the other passengers, her eyes skittering up and down the aisle. If the homely girl beside her was going to be foul-mouthed and obstinate, she would not let it dampen her spirits. She looked forward to these bus rides and managed at least one a year for the pure pleasure of meeting new faces. Not that there wasn't a good reason for her expedition—they were usually, like this one, for some meeting or General Conference of the Church or a wedding or a funeral—but she deliberately chose, as her husband would put it, "to fork out good money" for a bus trip, instead of taking advantage of a ride in one of the other ladies' cars, in order that—and this is something her husband never fully comprehended—she would not have to listen to—again, her husband's words—"the same old tune every time she took a notion to hightail it up north." The truth of the matter was, if she rode with Neola and LaPreal, she would have no recourse but to listen to Neola's harangue about MarDell's kids and Beverly's kids and Hartley's kids and their double promotions and various carryings-on. And if she caught a ride, as she had done on two different occasions, with Blair and R'Lene, she would be forced to sit through a replay of their trip to Hawaii, every detail of which she knew by now as well as they did, including the invariable recounting of how R'Lene turned her ankle at Haleakala, topped off by a few unavoidable renditions of "Pearly Shells." All Margene Savage could ever talk about, while *she* drove, was her hysterectomy, and neither Ardith nor Rolayne could think of anything but the La Leche League—as if she hadn't breast-fed all five of her own kids and without an organized troop of women to tell her how to do it.

She looked around her. Beside the thin sagging lady in the coat sat a teenaged Indian girl huddled in a Navajo blanket, and immediately Mrs. Winterrose thought of the project—entirely her own idea—that she was on her way to present to the ladies of the General Board in Salt Lake. Helping the Navajo sisters to find useful projects for the monthly Relief Society work meetings had always been a problem, but at last, she felt, she had hit upon an idea, and at two o'clock—a little less than sixteen hours from now, she calculated—she would be presenting it at the meeting. She sighed and looked around. Behind the Indian girl an old man snored with his mouth open, one leg sprawled diagonally in front of the empty seat so that a shoeless foot dangled into the aisle. It was after ten and most of the little overhead lights were off now, but, by hoisting herself up a little and squinting, Mrs. Winterrose could make out, in the seat behind the snoring man, a heavily made-up face under a platinum dome of ratted hair. The lady ("You can't kid me for a minute," Mrs. Winterrose assured herself. "That's no spring chicken hiding under that Max Factor mask!") was wearing dangling earrings that, from where Mrs. Winterrose sat, looked like the silver-and-turquoise kind sold in Indian curio shops, and they swung back and forth as the woman's platinum bubble bobbled around. Next to her, away from the window, was a thin girl with Bugs Bunny teeth and a tangerine-colored shell sweater. Across the aisle from them—Mrs. Winterrose had to crane her neck to see—seemed to be an empty seat; craning still further, she saw in the seat next to it a middle-aged fellow in a cowboy hat, his head against the window. Further back, though the lights were off there, she could see the boy in the denim jacket trying to get a look at the photos in the pocketbook of one of the girls while they half-whispered giggling squeals of protest and wrestled to get it back. Just behind her, and in front of the empty seat beside the cowboy, she could see, by twisting around the other way, a young couple in Levis and matching T-shirts, asleep with their heads braced against each other. Mrs. Winterrose glanced at the girl beside her who, evidently sensing it, twitched her mouth, turned and glared at her, then slapped the magazine closed and flung it down in the corner by her feet, heaved herself over to face the wall by the window, and pretended to go to sleep.

She was *not* going to be offended, Mrs. Winterrose decided. Because some unfortunate girl with a kinky permanent and a nasty tongue insisted on behaving like someone out of the state detention home, this was *not* going to spoil her whole trip. Besides, she refused to be shocked. The girl's behavior was not, after all, a revelation to her; she read the papers and went to the movies, didn't she? She had seen *The Bad Seed* and *Psycho* and heard enough about *Bonnie and Clyde* and *The Exorcist* to know what the score was. There were probably *some* people on the bus—and she took a moment to take another quick survey of her fellow passengers—who would have been totally devastated at such rude behavior. But there was only one way to get along in a world in which you never knew what you were going to run into next: patience, understanding, and a good listening ear. More than one young lady had bawled her heart out on Mrs. Winterrose's shoulder and she was no fool.

She looked around her. Not, she would have to admit, a very distinguished crew this trip. Once she had sat by a journalist from Nevada who was thinking of writing a screenplay on the Mountain Meadows Massacre. She twisted her neck around, saw again the empty seat beside the sleeping man in the cowboy hat, and suddenly rose up impulsively, giving one last "It's-your-loss-not-mine" glance to the scowling girl feigning sleep with one eye open, and situated herself in the empty seat two rows back.

"Too hot up there," she said, half aloud, waving a hand, fanlike, in front of her face. The man in the cowboy hat blinked his eyes, frowned, then smiled a perfunctorily cordial smile and closed his eyes again.

"You're not a journalist, are you?" she asked.

He blinked his eyes again and, squinting at her from under a half-scowl, turned his neck so that his head was tilted at an odd angle. "A which?"

"A writer. I mean, you look like you might be a writer or something."

He tipped his head still further so that he seemed to be viewing her almost horizontally through his still-squinting eyes. Then he laughed a long noiseless laugh, shaking his head. "Lady, I can't even spell."

Mrs. Winterrose felt nervous. "Well," she said, squaring up her purse on her lap, "that's nothing to be ashamed of. You look distinguished enough to be a writer, anyway—with those sideburns." Then she felt embarrassed for fear he would think she was being terribly forward, which she had never intended at all. "My husband," she quickly put in, "is very distinguished too—only in a different way." Why, what a lie, she told herself, picturing Deward out tending the calves. But she had had to say something. She was not sure that was enough, however; and she glanced at her old seat two rows ahead to make certain it was still empty, wondering what on earth she was doing back here in the first place. "He's more the—uh—Yul Brynner type," she went on, trying to gain composure. "Only older, of course."

He smiled dutifully again, but she had the impression he didn't know what she was talking about. She also feared he was about to go back to sleep, and decided to switch the subject. "Like horses, do you?"

He touched the brim of his hat and nodded.

"I was an extra in *Thunderhead*," she announced boldly, waiting to see his reaction.

He too seemed to be waiting. "You mean that big swanky night-club in Vegas?"

"No," she said quickly, mortified that he was picturing her in a line of plumed chorus girls waving their naked legs in the air. "With Preston Foster. My *Friend Flicka*, remember? Well, I was in *Thunderhead, Son of Flicka.*"

He scratched the back of his neck and shifted a little in his seat. "Yeah. I think I remember. Yeah. Dog, wasn't it?"

"Oh, no. Thunderhead was a horse." She was sorry he didn't remember, but then it occurred to her that he himself had prepared the ground for her next disclosure. "Now *Bob, Son of Battle*—that was a show about a dog," she said, trying not to sound overly excited. "With Lon McAllister and Peggy Ann Garner, remember? I was in *that* one, too."

His eyes actually grew larger, she felt. "You was actually in that?"

"Well," she said, "a small part. In the crowd."

"Well, I'll be a son of a gun," he said, nodding. "They called it *Lassie Come Home* or something like that, didn't they?"

She felt let down. "No, that was a different picture. I don't know where they made that. But *Thunderhead* and *Bob, Son of Battle* they made right here in Southern Utah."

He was still nodding, but she had the impression he was settling his head back against the window. "Yeah, well, I don't keep up much with most of that stuff."

"Now Roddy McDowell," she tried, "who was in *Lassie Come Home*, was the same one who starred in *Thunderhead*, along with Preston Foster. Now, if you remember *Lassie* or *Lad, Son of Lassie*, then—"

"No," he said, giving a cordial smile again, as he adjusted his hat and leaned back, "I don't think I seen it, neither. Just heard somethin' about it." Then he raised his head up. "You never was in any of them Roy Rogers or Gene Autry pictures, was you?"

"No," she said, feeling some regret. But before she could tell him about meeting Preston Foster in front of Bradshaw Auto Parts, he had already rested his head back and gone to sleep.

She watched from the window while a lone farmhouse passed by, a single light burning on its porch. Across the dark fields she could see a handful of lights sprinkled along the road that wound through the hills. That would be Hatch. She leaned back, listening to the low, steady hum of the bus. At least she had her meeting in Salt Lake City to think about. It made her feel good to think that the idea she was going to present to the ladies was all her own. And it really was a good idea. And useful too. She felt almost like an ambassador. Like Shirley Temple Black or someone.

When, later, the road seemed to dip down into the valley where the lights of Panguitch glimmered through the cottonwoods, she sat up and looked about her to see if anything had changed in case she had momentarily dozed. The girl with the rabbit teeth was fidgeting with her purse and some plastic bags as though she meant to get off, and somewhere up ahead a woman seemed to be trying to rouse a whimpering child as she stood swaying with the bus and pulling things from the rack overhead. The bus stopped at the end of the main street where only a street light and a pink neon sign that read Colonial Motel burned through the summer night. The driver got off and disappeared somewhere, followed by the girl with the rabbit teeth and another passenger from near the front. Then Mrs. Winterrose saw the lady from Fredonia get up and come waddling down the aisle toward her, but she merely nodded pleasantly as she passed by and motioned with her head that she was on her way to the restroom at the back of the bus. At the other end of the bus, the soldier was getting out, his hat still stuck under the strap on his shoulder, and she watched him from the window as he stood stretching under the street lamp. He would likely be heading home for the Fourth of July, she suspected—maybe to Richfield or to Gunnison or maybe even further north to Nephi or Spanish Fork. She was trying to think of the movie in which John Garfield had played a young soldier on leave when she noticed a man getting on, pushing his briefcase along in front of him as he came down the aisle.

He had a thin little moustache, and his hair, glistening with brilliantine, was combed back smoothly away from his high fore-head. He looked about him for a second, then moved back to the seat vacated by the girl with the long front teeth. He said something (that Mrs. Winterrose failed to catch) as he slipped in beside the blonde woman with the turquoise earrings, who acknowledged him with a slow smile and half-turn-of-the-head that reminded Mrs. Winterrose, against her will, of Rita Hayworth playing *Gilda*. She noticed that the woman wore black riding pants with a matching black Western shirt trimmed in purple.

"—ungodly hour for a bus ride," she heard the man say.

"At least it's cool, thank your luck stars for that," the woman answered, and Mrs. Winterrose bet herself that her eyelashes were false.

"It hasn't been any too hot in this burg," the man returned. He seemed to be sizing her up. "Where you from? Nevada?"

"Arizona," she said, giving her head a little music-hall wave and an extra chew to her gum. "Tucson."

"Going to Salt Lake?"

"American Fork. My husband's in the hospital there." To Mrs. Winterrose it seemed she paused to register his reaction. "Automobile accident. Completely totalled our car—a '74 Buick hardtop."

The man shook his head sympathetically, then pulled a package of gum out of his coat pocket and offered her a stick. Mrs. Winterrose was surprised to see her take one, but watched as she took out the gum that was already in her mouth and pressed it under the arm rest, then carefully unwrapped the new stick of Juicy Fruit and let it fold snakelike in her mouth.

"That blasted car of mine," the man was saying, "threw a rod clear out in the middle of nowhere, and I had to be towed all the way here. They could've fixed it for me if it wasn't for the blasted weekend and the Fourth coming up, but since I was going to have to be stuck here until Tuesday, I figured, what the heck, I might as well scoot on back up to Ogden—let the company pay for it."

Mrs. Winterrose's eyes dropped to his briefcase, which rested across his knees, and the woman in riding pants, too, stopped chewing her gum and motioned what seemed to Mrs. Winterrose to be an almost obscenely ringed hand toward it. "You a salesman?"

"Detail man," he answered. Used cars, Mrs. Winterrose bet herself. "Frozen foods," she heard him say.

A wail from up front startled her, and she was surprised to discover that the whimpering child and its mother had either returned to the bus or never left it. The woman was on her knees in the aisle poking and scraping under the seats where they had been sitting. The child had undoubtedly dropped something—a box of sparklers, Mrs. Winterrose decided, or a Fourth of July flag. She hoped the woman would find whatever it was and that the child would stop crying; it was difficult trying to pay attention to two things at once. The woman finally stood up, swept the child from the doorway of the bus, and got off just as the bus driver returned, followed by the soldier and some other passenger Mrs. Winterrose had missed. A quick glance at the empty seat up ahead, however, told her that the lady from Fredonia was still in the restroom or had gotten off to stretch her legs, and Mrs. Winterrose shifted to the edge of her seat and watched nervously from the window. The driver had already started the engine when the lady from Fredonia came bustling up the aisle, pulling at the back of her skirt and walking as though her feet hurt her. "Good grief," Mrs. Winterrose gasped to herself, noting a triangle of white hanging from the hem of the lady's skirt as she rocked up the aisle. "She's got a piece of toilet paper stuck to the back of her dress." Mrs. Winterrose felt it her duty to rise up and tell her, but the lady was already squeezing into her seat and the bus had started to lurch forward. She would have to remember to watch and see if it was still dangling there the next time she got up. The cowboy snored now beside her, and she turned back to the frozen foods salesman and the buxomy blonde in Western attire, irritated that she had missed out on so much of the conversation.

"—Errol Flynn?" she heard the gum-chewing blonde from Tucson say, and immediately she felt doubly cheated. She leaned her ear into the aisle.

"No," the salesman was saying, obviously flattered. "I can't say anybody ever did. It's probably this moustache," and he smoothed the thin dark line with his finger and thumb.

"Well, I was took for Lana Turner once, if you'd believe it."

No, thought Mrs. Winterrose, I certainly *wouldn't* believe it, but she stared hard at the woman to make sure that there was not some resemblance she had missed. There was not. Mae West, maybe, thought Mrs. Winterrose, but definitely *not* Lana Turner.

"—and everybody always said my little sister looked just like Shirley Temple, curly hair and all," the gum-chewing woman was saying, her turquoise earrings swinging. Shirley Temple, my foot, thought Mrs. Winterrose. If she had not been so polite she would have laughed out loud. I'll bet she's never seen Preston Foster face-to-face, she assured herself. She remembered how her own sister had even been considered as a stand-in for Peggy Ann Garner and probably would have been the one chosen too if Peggy Ann hadn't been quite so squatty.

"I knew a guy once," the salesman went on, "that was a dead ringer for Mickey Rooney. Used to ride the races over in Winnemucca when I was selling Wonder Bread."

"I wish you could've seen my first husband—Ronald Coleman to a T, moustache and all."

Mrs. Winterrose heard the cowboy beside her belch rudely and felt him shift himself more toward the window. She turned back to the salesman and the middle-aged blonde in the western outfit.

"He was a killer, this gorgeous wavy hair and all," the woman was going on. "But he wouldn't stop drinking for love nor money." She jabbed her ringed hand inside her shapeless purse and rummaged for a minute, then withdrew a handkerchief and dabbed at her nose and the corner of one of her painted eyes. Mrs. Winterrose held her breath, half-fearing, half-hoping to see one of the heavily mascaraed eyelashes topple off into the woman's lap, but nothing happened. "We was only married three years—three years and two months. I told him he was going to drink hisself to death and that's just exactly what he done. It affected his liver." She looked out of the window and jabbed again at her nose with the handkerchief. "Jeez, but he was beautiful."

Despite the dimness of the light, Mrs. Winterrose clearly saw the salesman reach over and place his hand on the ringed hand that rested on the purse. She shifted uneasily beside the sleeping cowboy and looked about her to see if anyone else was aware of what was taking place. A snicker from in front of her assured her that she was not alone, and she heard the boy whisper to his girlfriend something about "old Valentino over there." Mrs. Winterrose looked to see if the salesman had heard, but found him engrossed in whatever things he was whispering to the blonde woman beside him. It annoyed her that she could not even *hear* both of these conversations at once, let alone take part in them, and it occurred to her that she had not said a word yet to any of those around her, except to the sleeping cowboy and the rude girl with the frizzy hair, which hardly counted; yet she felt that she was a part of these other conversations nonetheless. And it was not as if she didn't have something to contribute.

The salesman had turned the light off overhead, and she realized that, except for a feeble glow coming from the front, the entire bus was now in darkness. From in front she heard snatches like "foot's gone to sleep" and "move your elbow just a little." Across the aisle the salesman was talking about "bowling" and "stock car races" and "Harrah's Club." Against her will, Mrs. Winterrose soon dozed. And she dreamed of *Thunderhead* and Preston Foster.

When she woke up, the bus was already at Manti. There seemed to be much shifting about, and she suddenly discovered that, not only had the Indian girl gotten off somewhere along the line, but the salesman and the blonde woman from Tucson were also getting out, and their seats were already being taken by two teenaged girls in Levis, one with her dark hair ratted under a reddish-brown wiglet held on by clippies, and the other with her thin blonde hair still up in curlers and her jaw working intently at the gum in her mouth. Mrs. Winterrose hoped the girl hadn't found it under the seat vacated by the woman from Tucson.

On further examination of the bus, she discovered that the soldier, too, was gone, and that the lady from Fredonia appeared to be asleep. Several people were trailing down the aisle to the bathroom and back, and a few others had gone outside to stretch, she noticed, but all seemed to be accounted for and back in their seats by the time the driver got in and started the motor—all, that it, except the frozen foods salesman and his Mae West friend. Mrs. Winterrose wanted to cry out for the bus driver to wait, that she was sure they had just gone to the other restroom inside or to buy more gum or something, but she didn't call out and he didn't wait and soon they were speeding down the highway in the blue-gray of the early morning.

Mrs. Winterrose sat back, decided to stop worrying, and surveyed the present situation. Beside her the cowboy, his Stetson now pulled down over his face, continued to sleep. Across the aisle, in front of the teenaged girls, the old man still snored, sprawled across two seats. Behind them, much to Mrs. Winterrose's surprise, sat a passenger that had evidently gotten on at Salina or Gunnison, escaping her notice—a striking older woman whose dark hair was pulled back into a sort of bun, exposing, on her ears, two tiny pearls. Here, Mrs. Winterrose recognized at once, was a lady of considerable refinement and, if the dim light was not playing tricks, a woman who even smiled amiably for a second when she turned her head and seemed to catch Mrs. Winterrose looking at her. Though she doubted how much the salesman's jockey friend had really resembled Mickey Rooney almost as much as she questioned any similarity, no matter how remote, between him and Errol Flynn (and, without question, between the buxomy blonde from Tucson and Lana Turner), there was no doubt here: this woman could have played Linda Darnell's mother any day—and without a stick of makeup. She took one glance at the hat of the cowboy, as if for approval, and then heaved herself up and slipped into the empty seat beside the woman two rows back.

"Too drafty over there," she said, scrunching up her nose and giving the other side of the bus a wave of her hand. The lady beside her turned her head slowly, gave a slight nod and the same congenial smile Mrs. Winterrose thought she had detected before, then continued to look straight ahead.

Mrs. Winterrose could hardly wait, as an opener, to tell her just exactly who she had put her in mind of, yet something made her decide at the last minute to hold off for a few seconds at least, and try a different approach. "Going north, are you?"

The older woman turned and smiled again, this time opening her lips as though to speak, yet she only shook her head slightly and wagged one finger in front of her face.

My land, thought Mrs. Winterrose, she's deaf and dumb. This was the second time this had happened to her on a ride to Salt Lake: four years ago or so, it had been a young student-looking fellow that had looked at first glance just as intelligent as anyone else. Embarrassed, Mrs. Winterrose regretted she had never learned to make at least some simple apologetic statement in sign language, but then saw the lady pull something from her purse and decided she was probably going to write her a message. That, she told herself, would be the most unique conversation she had ever held on a bus, but she supposed it could be done, although it might be a little difficult trying to say anything very casually when you had to print it right out like it was a matter of life and death. I HAVE SEEN PRESTON FOSTER FACE TO FACE just didn't seem like something you would slip to a total stranger on a scrap of paper, and it embarrassed Mrs. Winterrose further that she had even thought of it.

The paper, however, that the woman held out to her seemed at first to make no sense whatsoever:

Maria Concepcion Garcia-Rojas
Lavina S. Fugal Hall
Brigham Young University
Provo, Utah 84602

But then she became aware that the woman was actually talking—that she was patting her arm to get her attention and pointing her other hand toward her breast and saying what sounded to Mrs. Winterrose like "Me, Ninny," raising her eyebrows at the same time in a sort of uncertain frown as if waiting to be assured that Mrs. Winterrose understood, which she most certainly did not. The lady found something else in her purse—a snapshot of a pretty girl with short dark hair standing in front of a fountain—and then ran her finger along the name on the card she had shown her earlier, saying again, slowly and deliberately, the funny foreign words that Mrs. Winterrose was beginning to take for Spanish.

"Oh," Mrs. Winterrose said quite loudly, suddenly feeling she was on the verge of receiving the gift of tongues, yet noticing at the same time that two or three people had turned around to look back at her. "It's her daughter," the cowboy said, removing his hat from his face long enough to speak. "Oh," Mrs. Winterrose said again, somewhat more quietly, feeling compelled to rock a make-believe child in her arms to put her point across. The lady tried to smile but looked confused, so Mrs. Winterrose just patted her arm and nodded as vigorously as she could, summoning up her "Just-you-leave-everything-to-me" smile. But then it occurred to her that her gift of tongues definitely had its limitations and, whether her foreign passenger-friend was deaf and dumb or not, her own knowledge of sign language was somewhat feeble and she certainly couldn't carry on much of a conversation repeating "Vaya con Dios" or "Rio Rancho Grande." For a few minutes she just stared straight ahead,

wishing she had gone to the bathroom earlier, then she felt compelled to turn to the lady, smile again and give her arm another pat
or two and then look straight forward for a few more miles.

It was still partly dark outside when the bus pulled up in front of
the D. & S. Service in Mount Pleasant and Mrs. Winterrose saw the
cowboy get off, followed by the boy in the denim jacket who waved,
grinning from the sidewalk, to the girls on the back seat as they
waved back exaggeratedly through the window and mouthed giggling last-minute messages to him. The only passenger to get on was
a tall elderly woman, her thin, white, marcelled finger-waves held
close to her pink scalp by an army of gray bobby pins. Nodding her
head and smiling at everyone as she came down the aisle, she finally
situated herself and a paper sack that smelled of hard-boiled eggs in
the seat abandoned by the cowboy. She leaned back only for a
moment, however; then, looking around her, she grasped the back
of the seat in front of her and scooted herself to the edge of the seat
nearest the aisle where, with an encompassing glance, she seemed to
address herself to them all:

"Well, you couldn't ask for much more perfect weather than
this, could you?"

Mrs. Winterrose smiled and nodded in agreement while she
tried to think whether it really had been too hot or too cold, and
the elderly woman inclined herself forward and continued: "I'm on
my way to Salt Lake City—to go in the Mission Home."

The two girls in the seat across from her stopped chewing their
gum and gaped at her.

"You didn't know they called people my age on a mission, did
you?" she said proudly, addressing the girls as she might have done a
Junior Sunday School class. "Well, they did, me and my husband
both. And Rell," she confided, "is going to be seventy-one on
Armistice Day." She pursed her lips together as if awaiting their
reaction.

"Imagine that," Mrs. Winterrose said, and the girls looked back
at her and then went on chewing their gum. The girl in curlers,
chewing vigorously, kept letting hers poke out through her teeth
and occasionally stretched it thin over her tongue as if trying to
blow a bubble.

"We're going to the Minnesota-Minneapolis Mission," the lady

103

went on, "and that includes Minnesota, Wisconsin, and Michigan."
She looked directly at the woman who looked like Linda Darnell's
mother, and Mrs. Winterrose noticed that the woman smiled back
although she couldn't possibly have understood a word.

"Is that anywhere by Oklahoma?" the girl in the wiglet and
lavender eye shadow asked. "I know this kid that's in the army
there."

"No," the lady said, seeming to take care not to offend. "No,
that would be one of your midwestern states missions, I suspect. No,
ours is all those northern states, and oh, my, they tell me it can get
cold. Rell's got to get him a new overcoat, and he's so busy taking
our watering turn and looking after this new mare we got that's got
a big welt on her hind leg that he's leaving it all up to me to pick it
out and everything, and he's going to either get him a ride or drive
on up in the pickup early Tuesday morning."

"This kid in Oklahoma's been everywhere. Denver and just
about any place you can imagine." She popped her gum. "He thinks
that when he comes home in December I'm going to marry him, but
if he thinks I'm just going to sit around and twiddle my thumbs
until then, he's got another think coming."

"Oh, my, I should say so," the lady said. "You wouldn't want to
be getting married to anybody at your age."

"She'd marry anything in pants," said the blonde with the
curlers, and Mrs. Winterrose heard the other girl slap her on the leg.

"Well," said the elderly woman, brushing from her lap what
seemed to Mrs. Winterrose to be some imaginary crumbs, "I've got
me a full schedule today and tomorrow, I can tell you that, what
with the Fourth and all, and all the stores being closed on Monday."

"This girlfriend of mine knows of a girl in Ohio or Iowa or one
of those places that was walking home from school in broad day-
light and got raped in a vacant lot."

"Well," the elderly lady went on, tipping her head to pat at the
even waves secured by the bobby pins behind her ear, "I always say
you just have to try to see the beautiful and the good in everything.
There's an awfully lot of good people in this world and—"

"Blacked both of her eyes and broke her nose and left her bleeding right there in a heap of tin cans and old broken bottles."

"—you just have to try to do what you know is best no matter what the rest of the world thinks. There's one thing I've always said, and that's if you can't say something good about somebody—"

"There's a lot of people though," put in the blonde, "that deserves to be put in the state penitentiary. There's nothing good you can say about *them*, like this guy that used to work for my gramma and carted off her washing machine that was only about a year old—"

"Well," said the marcelled lady, "I always said that if you always try to look for the good, you're sure to find it. My mother used to say to me, 'Euphora, some folk are bound and determined to look for the thorns in life while others are just as content as you please to enjoy the roses.'" She looked to Mrs. Winterrose and to the dark lady for approval. But the girl in the wiglet and the eye shadow hoisted her Levied legs up into the seat so that, kneeling, she now faced the missionary lady directly.

"What would you think," she said, narrowing her eyes, "if *your* best friend went and blabbed all over town that you was smoking and drinking, and it was just a great big dirty rotten lie?"

"I've never touched a cigarette," the lady said, unruffled, addressing them all, "nor tasted a single drop of alcohol. And what's more," she added, "I've never cared to."

"Coca-Cola is just as bad or worse than coffee," put in the blonde, shaking her curlers. "My sister, y'know, used to just love these big fat Hershey bars—the kind with all these nuts and stuff—and then after a while her face broke out and she was just *covered* with all these pimples. She had to keep this awful stuff on her face, I don't know what it's called, but she used to try to hide it by putting on just layers and layers of this gucky makeup and—"

Mrs. Winterrose suddenly wanted to tell them how Preston Foster looked in his everyday clothes without a stick of makeup, but already the elderly woman was advising them of the best way to get to know someone, and the girl in the curlers had started off on what kind of a mess the cleaners had made of her new formal. It was going to be next to impossible, Mrs. Winterrose could see, to ever get a chance to get anything in about *Bob, Son of Battle* or *Thunderhead* either one on this trip with the rest of them talking a mile a minute and acting as if she and the dark lady *both* were totally deaf and dumb.

By the time the bus pulled in behind the bus depot in Provo, the sun was just beginning to make the sky pink behind the mountains, and after she got up to let the dark foreign lady out and then stood in line for her turn in the restroom, Mrs. Winterrose decided that she might as well ride the rest of the way into Salt Lake sitting by the lady from Fredonia.

They had a nice enough chat. Not that the lady from Fredonia had anything all that interesting to say, or that Mrs. Winterrose herself ever got a chance to talk about most of the things that she really wanted to, but they did chat some about the usefulness of learning a few words in sign language, and also talked at some length about the need there was in the world to really try to understand others. Once when the conversation seemed on the verge of veering in a direction that made Mrs. Winterrose sit up straight, tingling, in her seat, the lady from Fredonia admitted right off that she "couldn't tell one movie star from another," and what was more, she had scarcely been to two movies in all her married life and, if she remembered right, they were both *Gone with the Wind*.

And so it was a long ride, all in all, to Mrs. Winterrose, and when she finally got off in Salt Lake City, she felt a little dissatisfied, a little cheated. There was a lot, she felt, locked up inside of her that never had a chance to get out. And so she was glad, when she thought about it, that she had a meeting to go to, something to take her mind off the disappointed feeling that squirmed inside her. It boosted her spirits somewhat to remember that at two o'clock she was going to tell the ladies her idea about teaching the Navajos in her area how to make rag rugs out of plastic bags. And there was always the chance—although she couldn't for the life of her imagine how it would ever come up—that, *somehow*, maybe if they found out where she was from, someone *might* just ask_____. But she would try her best not to think about that, for the moment.

Homecoming

"I just keep having this feeling that something terrible is going to happen," she had told him. It was a sort of premonition, she had said—which was odd because, unlike his mother, she never claimed premonitions or hunches and even admitted that, if there was such a thing as "woman's intuition," she had never felt it.

Glade had at first attributed her reluctance to go to the fact that she would have to miss club and the children's swimming lessons would be interrupted; later it struck him that she might be dreading a full week in the house with his mother: each time they had visited during the last eleven years, the always unspoken tension had seemed increasingly more likely to erupt. He remembered the last trip home, three summers before, when, despite a scarcely healed broken hip, his mother had insisted on supervising the dishwashing ritual and had constantly presided over the stove, substituting pans and resetting the burner knobs and, as Bernice had expressed it to him later, forever insinuating by her mumbled "I usually do this" and "I always do that" that *her* ways, the old familiar tried-and-true ways, were the best.

But it wasn't *that*, Bernice claimed when he finally brought the idea out in the open; it was just a terrible feeling she had that some doom was waiting somewhere in the blur of summer-hot days that lay nebulously ahead of them out there in the West, that maybe they shouldn't try to go back at all—at least not now. He decided then that it was probably just their different backgrounds finally rubbing and grating against one another: she had been from Cleveland, after all—a nurse he had met skiing one February during her two-week vacation in Vail, Colorado. Her interest in skiing, she openly admitted later, had been far less substantial than her interest

110

in the young men reputedly congregated at such resorts during the winter weekends, and, having found and married one of them, she admitted as well that she was quite frankly still a city girl at heart and that she had been relieved when Glade's eventual MBA degree at Ohio State and an interview with General Motors had finally maneuvered them back East—although neither Newark nor Rochester nor even Detroit, she again admitted, would have been her first choice.

But Panguitch, Utah (population 1,318), was another matter—he knew that from the way she had endured his relatives and old friends on those previous encounters, brief and far between, strung out here and there during the past eleven years. Bernice always had at her disposal a teeth-gritting smile for certain obligations. Even without her "premonition"—or whatever label he would finally put on it—she would probably have preferred a week in the other direction—Martha's Vineyard or Cape Cod, or south to Washington, D.C., Williamsburg, Miami, or New Orleans. But home, to Glade, was home—at least he liked to think that—and three years without going back to see his family, without being able to walk out behind the house under the trees or wander down some of the old familiar streets seemed a long time, far too long. Each time they had gone back, he had fully intended to take a walk up through the cottonwoods around the Airdome or to borrow a bicycle from somewhere and see what it felt like to pedal once again down the long tree-lined road that led to Roller-Mill Hill and the grove of cottonwoods and willows along the river. But somehow it had never worked out: once it had been a cold and windy February; and the last time, although the weather had been right, he had spent each day either in the basement or the garage helping his father sort out box after box of odds and ends from the past. There had been at least one other time besides that—a few days in the late June or July, because he remembered that the yellow roses were already out; yet something even then had prevented him from finally taking those little excursions he always thought about while he was away, but he couldn't remember now exactly what it had been.

Now, once again, the shady little town of his past seemed to draw him; and he could almost feel its magnetic pull growing in proportion to Bernice's hesitancy. There were times when her doubts—

"I just keep having this feeling that maybe we shouldn't go"—even seemed to be rubbing off on him, the way a chain or a watchband sometimes begins to leave a mark, a faint discoloration on the skin, but he fought against it. "Look," he had told her, assuring himself as well as her, "we don't need to break our necks getting there: we can take two or three days for the drive instead of just one, if you'd feel better. After all, there's no real rush—we'll still have almost a full week after we get there anyway. And we'll both keep our eyes on the kids—if it's the irrigation ditches you're worried about." It would be a relief this year, he had thought to himself several times, just knowing that the three children were older—Grant, nine; Doug, seven; and Shelley now almost five; three summers before both Bernice and his mother had worried about them every second they were outside.

But there was something ironic about it all: in many ways, he had come to feel over the years much the same way about the little town as Bernice did—that it was a long way from nowhere, that there was next to nothing for the young people or anyone else to do, that his friends had all moved away and now even the few relatives that still straggled on seemed to have little in common with them any more; and yet, her attitude this summer—her reluctance, even her "intuitions"—had somehow, strangely, made him feel all the more intently the desire, the *need*, to go.

And so they went. Taking their time through the Midwest but gradually pushing harder by the time they reached Nebraska and Wyoming, they crossed the Utah state line shortly after noon of the third day and drove straight through, bypassing Salt Lake and Provo and hurrying on south until the old familiar landmarks of Junction, Circleville, and Spry gave way to the open stretch of sagebrush where, as the road turned east, the houses of Panguitch were sprinkled among the trees. But, to Glade, there was something just a little disturbing even before the houses or the trees were fully visible. From five or six miles out, he had begun to notice the strange gray smoke billowing up above the horizon and blotting out the low blue hills beyond; and it was not until they had almost reached the edge of town that he remembered the sawmill and how, although it had been there for some time now, and his father had mentioned it off and on in letters throughout the years since he had left home, it could always give him a little jolt, on returning, to find it there like some strange intruder on the world he thought he knew so well.

And as they finally rounded the slight curve where the old cheese factory had once been, and he saw the space left by the two-story brick home where, time after time, he had gone on his bicycle to buy fresh curd, he felt a quick little tightening in his stomach. He glanced back over his shoulder: the race track seemed to still be there, even the weathered grandstand, but many of the trees were gone and the old stables had been removed. And when he saw the spot vacated by the old Rose-a-Rena where, on summer nights, rollicking organ music had sent laughing roller-skaters sailing around the pink open-air enclosure to the tunes of "Cruising Down the River" and "Powder Your Face with Sunshine," he felt again the clenching within. There were more motels than he remembered, more even than the summer three years before, and most of them now, their neon signs dormant in the August afternoon sun, boasted TV and swimming pools. Television, he recalled, had been a long time coming to Panguitch, not arriving, in fact, until after he had gone away to college; and the nearest swimming pool, small and cold even in mid-summer, had been in Richfield, almost two hours up the long road that led to Salt Lake City.

"Hey, Dad, look—!" Grant was saying, leaning over the seat. "Swimming pools. I thought you told us—"

About the Flume—a widening in the canal beyond Roller-Mill Hill where water snakes had zigzagged harmlessly in the milky brown water; where white skinny bodies, laughing and splashing in the sunlight, would return to the bank to find their clothes pirated away or tied in knots beneath the willows; and where, on "dog days," mothers warned, snakes might bite at anything. And at dusk the moist green smell of willow branches stripped of their gray bark and pierced through a fat weiner that would burst and sizzle over the red coals while the woody smoke drifted up through the trees—

"Look, Dad—stop! There's a drive-in!" Doug cried out. "Can we get a hot dog or something? They've got slushes too!"

A Frost-Top, surrounded by cars. He tried to remember what had been there before. Maybe another one of the old brick houses, two or three stories tall, with round cupolas, white gingerbread trimming the porch and gables, and stained glass windows . . . His fingers, on the steering wheel, felt numb. They were passing a flat piece of grassless ground marked TRAILER PARK on the left; on the right, a new low building with the sign MOBILE HOME SALES.

"How come we didn't stop?" Shelley whined, her voice sharp with four-year-old incredulity. "Can't we get a cherry slush? Or an orange freeze?"

Not now, he told her, since Grandma was expecting them and probably had something all prepared; but his mind ran on: cherry slushes and orange freezes—why weren't they right? Fresh lemonade and Oreo cookies under the lilac trees. Nabisco sugar wafers and Crackerjacks. And under the weeping willow, beside the hammock with the stack of fifteen-cent *Classics Illustrated* and the Big-Little Books of *Flash Gordon* and *Our Gang*, a cool pitcher of lime Kool-Aid. And on summer afternoons when the big fan in the Panguitch drugstore revolved slowly on the high ceiling and the flypaper hung down in ochre spirals, he had spun himself around on the soda-fountain stools, waiting for the tall lady behind the counter to ·release a thick stream of orange crush from the frosted-glass bubble, or to pull down the handle that spurted a fizzling shaft of carbonated water into the thick dark syrup that would become Ironport or that surprising mixture of flavors with a squirt of sour that was called Wild Horse and never tasted the same way twice. Dixie Cups for a nickle, Happy Days for a dime. And for a quarter, a silver container supporting a white paper cone full of vanilla ice cream and black-walnut syrup, topped with marshmallow, malt powder, and crushed nuts, a thin triangular wafer stuck in the top. And behind the glass showcase trimmed with brown wood, the rows of five-cent chocolate bars called Denver Sandwich, Chicken Dinner, O Henry, and Old Nick; the pastel-colored paper-wrapped Guess Whats, the Walnettoes and Carmelloes, the thin paper envelopes of Sen-Sens, the sugary watermelon slices beside the wax moustaches, teeth, and red lips, and the tiny wax bottles filled with sweet syrup—red, purple, and green.

"Hey, they've got another drive-in too, Dad—"

"Maybe tomorrow," Bernice hushed them.

The second drive-in, now enlarged and remodeled, had been there three years ago, maybe even several years before that; but it still hadn't been part of the old town, part of his memories. There had been a tiny hamburger place near the school run by two grandmothers and called The Ru-Mil, and years before that, a very narrow one called The Shack, wedged between the old jewelry store and the Southern Utah Equitable, where two young brothers had sold root beer from a keg and along the street you could hear the juke box playing "Jeepers, Creepers" and "Beer Barrel Polka."

The Blue Pine Hotel. He felt himself smile. At least something was still there. But the green movie theater across the street—"the show house," they had called it—was boarded up, its marquee naked; and further down the little block called Main Street, disguised by a large plateglass facade, the drugstore had a large sign on the door: EXCUSE THE MESS: SODA FOUNTAIN BEING REMOVED.

Bernice touched his arm as he turned the station wagon sharply to the left. "I have the hardest time imagining you growing up here," she said quietly, half smiling. "I try to picture it but I can't."

"It was almost a different place then," he heard himself saying aloud, noticing a new bowling alley and, further on, where Tom's Cabins had been, a parking lot stretched out before a cinderblock supermarket. He glanced up the street to the right; behind a few low trees the smoke from the sawmill discolored the sky. He turned left, almost nervously trying to absorb everything that passed by on both sides of the street.

"You mean it was bigger?" Grant wanted to know, leaning over the seat. "Or smaller?"

"About the same, actually. But quite different." He could see already that the old multistoried elementary school had been taken down. He felt again the sudden tightening in his stomach. A new school, small and flat, baked in the sun on the empty lot. All of the houses now, he noticed, seemed different, starker; many had aluminum awnings, and some had had their porches glassed in.

"Did they have cars and stuff then?"

"Of course they had cars!" Bernice answered, her voice almost indignant. "Good grief, how old do you think we are?"

"I did ride my bike a lot though," Glade found himself saying, feeling uneasy that Grant's initial question still went unanswered. The trees—that was part of it. Most of the cottonwoods, he noticed, had been cut down on each side of the street. Even the old picket fences were missing. And Guymonds' weeping willow. They passed a lot, vacant except for a small mobile home supporting a massive TV antenna.

"Does Grandma still have your bike?"

"I can't remember. I think we sold it. But maybe we can borrow a bike or two and ride out toward the cemetery or—"

Bernice squeezed his arm. "Please, not the cemetery," she whispered between her teeth. "That's all I need."

He saw her fold her arms and run her hands up and down her upper arms as if to warm them, as he brought the car to a stop in front of the house where he had lived for almost twenty years.

"Is this it?" Shelley asked, her voice all but drowned out in Doug and Grant's jubilant "We're here!"

"This is it," he said. But was it really? Was it really what he had been aching to come home to? The fence was gone as well as the big trees that had shaded the lot; the tall brick house, sheared of its vines, now seemed to jut up, stark and almost forlorn, out of the flat rectangle of trimmed grass. He turned away.

"Still having those feelings?" he asked quietly, hearing Bernice sigh and resting his hand on her knee. If she answered, it was lost under the squeals of the three in the back, but he saw her give a nervous little nod. The back door of the station wagon was flung open, and Shelley was already trailing behind Grant and Doug as they scrambled up the steps to see who could get to the front door first. In a moment his mother was there on the porch with them, her hair, evidently in pincurls, covered by a tulle cap with what seemed to be pink cloth roses stuck on it. He saw her bend down, with difficulty, to let the children give her a hug, then straighten up, as best she could, and pat at her head with both hands. "You'll think you've got the funniest grandma in the world," he could hear her telling the kids as he and Bernice started up the walk. He could picture her, long ago, heavier, more rosy-cheeked, her pincurls hidden under a flowered bandana, sitting on the porch shelling peas from the garden or weeding sweetpeas and pansies along the south side of the house.

"Why, shame on you kids for staying away for so long," she scolded, giving them each a peck on the cheek and squeezing their arms. "I think Dad's fallen asleep in front of the TV," she said, partly smiling. "He likes to catch the five o'clock news. Me, I've been kinda waiting and watching out of the window for you all afternoon."

Glade hesitated while she held the storm door open, ushering them all into the house. The door was wrong. What had happened to the old door with the stained-glass hexagon? And the old screen door. He glanced off to the right where the green and white porch swing had once hung. One of the rings, rusted now, still hung from the ceiling. Below, in place of the swing, were two dusty aluminum chaise lounges with orange webbing.

"Daddy," his mother called from the hall into the living room. "Glade and Bernice are here." Shelley hung back in the doorway, but Grant and Doug marched on in to where their grandfather was rousing himself from the sofa. Some of the furniture, Glade noticed, was new; the flowered drapes had been replaced by some neutral ones, steel-colored, and a speckled gray carpet, wall to wall, took the place of the floral-patterned rug he remembered.

"Well, aren't you a sight for sore eyes!" his father was saying to Shelley, then he was stretching out both of his arms and gathering both Glade and Bernice to him.

"Handsome as ever," Bernice told him, giving the wrinkled cheek a playful pat. "It's great to be home, Dad," Glade found himself saying, knowing that neither statement, his nor Bernice's, was totally true. For years now he had winced at the evidences of old age encroaching upon his mother; now, for the first time, he saw his father as an old man, his thick hair grown suddenly very gray, his eyes sunken now and clouded.

"Well, how does the old town look to you?" Glade heard him ask. "Notice anything different from the front yard out there?"

The trees. He wanted to ask him about the row of cottonwoods gone from along the south side and in front of the house. He wanted to ask about the vines—and about the birch. Suddenly he knew it was gone too. It might have even been gone the last time they came, yet somehow the old memories had crowded in again, pushing out the things he didn't want to acknowledge.

"What happened to the vines?" He hadn't decided whether to bring it up or not, but there it was.

"Oh, I had Elmo Lambert and old DeLane what's-his-name

help me take 'em down two or three years ago. Why, those dang things had pret-near covered every inch of the house—"

"I remember."

"—windows, TV antenna, and all."

"I noticed you took out the cottonwoods, too. And the birch."

"We should've had those cottonwoods took out a heck of a long time ago, nuisance that they were. Do you remember how that cotton used to blow around here every summer—"

Like the smell of sweet peas or the taste of raw rhubarb, freshly cut, out of the garden. Like the scent of bridal wreath or plum blossoms out behind the house, or the dizzying fragrance of lilacs along the back fence. Like the sunflowers and hollyhocks eight feet high or the yellow roses that looked and smelled like July. Like them, the cotton, too, had been summer, tickling across his cheek and nose while he lay on his back on the clover and dandelions, watching the clouds change shape in the blue overhead, or as he sat barelegged on a log fallen across the river, dazzled by the water rushing beneath him while he let his feet dangle in its icy freshness.

"—and that old birch was just as good as dead anyway. Elmo cut it down, and then I had him burn the stump out and get rid of it. Makes it a whole lot nicer—"

"Anybody hungry?" his mother broke in, standing in the kitchen doorway. "I'll bet you're all starving to death. Did you folks ever try these Swanson TV dinners? Dad, he likes the chicken best, but I'd just as leave have the ham or one of the others. Come in and pick out whatever—"

For a second he saw in his mind the old kitchen table with the yellow- and white-checkered oilcloth. It would be gone now, along with the little white stool and the yellow and green linoleum, gone with the whole string of summer evenings when they would sit around the table at suppertime watching through the open door the nighthawks swooping through the twilight sky. The bowls of bread and milk, the dishes of yellow-green currants bathed in cream and sugar, the big plate heaped with fresh radishes and green onions just pulled from the garden and the dark green watercress brought home from along the ditchbank in the pasture—what had become of it all? It was gone like the milk separator and the butter churn, like the long thin cooler with wire-mesh shelves where the butter and cheese

118

were once kept and he could stick his head inside and look all the way down to the cellar where irregular bottles of homemade root beer stood in rows among the bottled cherries and pickled beets. And the gray cardboard pictures from between the layers of Nabisco's Shredded Wheat hoarded in the bottom cupboard with the empty cabin-shaped cans that had once held Log Cabin syrup— what had happened to them? And the frosty Saturday mornings, eating a bowl of hot mush at the table with the windows all steamed up while the little radio on the shelf sang "Cream of Wheat is so good to eat" and transformed the winter mornings with the magic of *Let's Pretend* . . .

"Do you think maybe little Shelley could eat a whole frozen turkey dinner all by herself?"

And so for over an hour they sat in the kitchen with its new dinette set and indoor-outdoor carpeting, eating the TV dinners and talking while the light grew grayer and grayer outside.

By nine o'clock, Glade was relieved that Bernice had slipped away to get the kids ready for bed, when his mother announced suddenly, "Oh, Glade. Poor old Milo Lister is dead. Remember him? Had that little bit of a house way down by the River Lane? Valdean walked in and found him dead on the kitchen floor yesterday morning."

"Either a stroke or a heart attack," his father said.

"That makes two," she went on, looking at him knowingly. "Orrin Sudweeks' wife died last week with cancer."

Suddenly he knew what she meant, and a little shiver snaked down his spine. Panguitch folk had always talked about death in threes: if someone died, two more were sure to follow within a few days. The superstition struck him as more foolish now than ever; yet it bothered him to think that he couldn't recall a single time in all his years of growing up that it hadn't happened just that way.

"You want to watch that little girl of yours," his mother went on. "And the boys too, for that matter. Erland Ferguson took his youngest boy hunting jackrabbits last spring, and the gun went off in the pickup and shot him. And one of Wilma Dalton's grandkids was run over by one of those big old semitrucks right in front of the Flying M. I tell you, it just worries you to death."

She got up from the table and stood for a moment in front of

119

the sink. "I don't know what we've done to be so lucky." She said it almost to herself, and Glade could sense her next words even before she said them. "Knock on wood," she sighed, giving the wooden drainboard a little rap with her bony knuckles. That was so like her, Glade thought: sprinkling salt over her left shoulder, refusing to shake a tablecloth after dark, knowing someone was talking about her whenever she heard a ringing in her ears—ideas she would probably try to laugh at if you questioned her, yet habits that were part of her nonetheless.

"We'll have to take Glade and Bernice out and let them get a look at our new cemetery," she was saying, taking the dishes from the table.

"*New* cemetery?" Glade asked.

"She means the old one," his father answered. "They've done quite a little bit of fixing up out there since you probably saw it last. They took out all of them old trees and put in some nice grass. They leveled it all off first and—"

Glade remembered the row of cottonwoods that lined the little lane leading to what they had called "the graveyard." A smell, strangely mixed, suddenly came back to him: lilacs and carnations wedded with the smoke from burning tumbleweeds. As a child, along with the whole town, he had kept the yearly ritual of going to the graveyard on Decoration Day at the end of May, and he remembered now the all-day task as families raked and burned the weeds and leaves and chatted with friends and neighbors over the graves. Tired of raking, he would terrorize ant hills for a while and then wander off, taking care to walk softly among the smooth headstones, some blue-gray and some sparkling white, sometimes daring to run his hand over the woolly lambs and babies' shoes and books whose marble pages would never turn. In the afternoon, they would sit, in families, under the shade of the big trees, eating the tuna-fish sandwiches and macaroni salad and slices of the dark chocolate hot-water cake kept cool under a dish towel in a "dripper" pan.

"—these California outfits come in here and try to buy up all the land," his father was saying. "They're gathering up anything that's loose and don't seem to care what they have to pay to get it. Even out at the cemetery. And you should see what they've done to the lake. First it was the CCC camps, then those Hollywood movie outfits. Every dang one of those resorts up there has been taken over by some Californian that came in here and knew a good thing when he saw it."

The lake. Pinenuts and pine gum. Winding through the scrub pine and then following the creek through the meadows and up the side of the mountain above the gorge until the road finally dipped down and rounded a curve and there it was. In summers, the whole town had seemed to move up there, trading stories and shouting happy hellos as they passed one another going down to the boats or on their way to the well to fill their buckets with water. Beyond Sharpwalker Bay, the cream-colored rocks had been like crystal, and behind the cabins the hillsides had been full of arrowheads and Indian paintbrush. Through the pines again and across a meadow to the edge of the shimmering green quaking aspen and there, with deer trails leading to it, was Blue Spring, bluer than you ever remembered, and clear and icy cool when you drank it from your hands.

"Poor Glade," his mother cut in, her voice tired but affectionate. "Here we are talking your leg off, and you probably can't wait to get to sleep. I should think you'd be so worn out from all that driving that you wouldn't give a hoot about the lake or the cemetery either one." She put her bony hand on his shoulder. "The upstairs bedroom's all made up for you folks. Tomorrow you can worry about getting reacquainted."

He remembered her words almost immediately when he opened his eyes early the next morning. Getting reacquainted did worry him a little—*more* than a little—and he felt even more sure of this as he lay quietly in bed beside Bernice, letting his eyes drift over the pastel-painted walls, wanting to see through the layer of paint to the wallpaper that he knew was still there, wallpaper whose pale green-and-gold florid pattern had once let him imagine he could make out peacocks and flying horses and fantastic faces and shapes. On summer mornings long ago he had lain in bed watching the sunlight coming through the vines and projecting a lively shadow-play on the opposite wall as the breeze lightly ruffled the leaves. The light sneaking through the curtains now, no longer impeded by vines, cast only a hard distorted rectangle on the wall across the room.

A glance at his watch told him it was still very early. He lay for a moment without moving; then, feeling a sudden urge to wander by himself around the yard before anyone else awakened, he slipped quickly out of bed, put on his clothes and a jacket, and quietly went downstairs and let himself out of the front door.

The yard was still. A pickup rattled down the street and then the street too was quiet. Only a steady grinding noise from far away broke the morning stillness. Slowly he stepped off the porch and started down the front walk, then turned away suddenly toward the few remaining lilac trees along the north side of the house; with the front fence gone and all the cottonwoods removed, there was a starkness, a certain threatening glare, that he didn't like to think about. Once long ago, he remembered, he had drowsed here in a green wooden box-swing, listening to the tinkling sounds of "Nola" and the "Whistling Waltz" coming from the player-piano next door and watching the warm afternoon light as it filtered down through the big green leaves in shifting patterns. He moved now toward the back of the house. The bridal wreath was gone, and no flowers grew along the side of the house where gladiolas and chrysanthemums had been. He bent down, trying to peer in the low basement window that, though once almost obscured by vines, was now just a darkened, dust-streaked rectangle at the base of the house. Inside, a few old boxes seemed to be stacked almost window-high. If he searched among them all, could he find what he wanted, could he bring any of it back? He doubted that the old costume trunk would still be there, waiting with its treasure of chintz and crepe paper to transfigure ordinary little boys and girls into bluebirds and elves. If lucky, in some stray box he might find one or two yellow-incrusted test tubes, remnants from his chemistry set, but how could he bring back the smells, the sounds, the feel of those days?

Behind the house he found that the plum trees had been cut back until only two or three of them still straggled against the back fence. The fence itself had been replaced by a wire one, and the spot where the garden had been was now just an empty lot with an old refrigerator and some bald tires stacked in one corner. He looked back at the few remaining plum trees. Once this had seemed a massive green jungle; how many summer afternoons had he spent there rescuing Dorothy Lamour or echoing Johnny Weismuller's primitive call? He looked up, half expecting to see remains of his treehouse, but even the Chinese elm itself was gone. Summer after summer he had strained for heights, relishing the view as he peered down from treehouse slats, from barn-loft windows, from home-made stilts of boards or tin cans. Now, however, he felt uncomfortably tall, the surroundings truncated, dwarfed, exposed.

The flat empty space where the sunflowers and hollyhocks had bordered the garden bothered him, and he felt a little gnawing feeling in the pit of his stomach. Whenever he had thought about home over the years, the picture that came was almost always one of summertime and grass-stained knees: pulling up a turnip or a stalk of rhubarb from the garden to eat raw in the shade of the trees; chasing hummingbirds, butterflies, and dragonflies, or running away from devil's darning-needles that were supposed to sew your mouth shut; and in the summer dark, crawling close to the fresh-smelling grass with a flashlight, searching for the wiggly night-crawlers to sell for bait to the fishermen; and, later, watching the fireflies, listening to the crickets, and smelling the night grass while sleeping out under the big willow and waiting for the tremble of cannons to bring in the Fourth of July.

He started across the lawn and stopped. Long ago, on warm summer evenings, they had played croquet under the willow tree and around the bushes of bridal wreath. And sometimes they had strung colored lights from tree to tree and set up long tables full of food for parties at night to which it seemed the whole town was invited. On other nights, for the kids in this end of town, there had been a lot of scrambling over fences and lying breathless in the dark beneath the lilac bushes while someone cried out, from far away, "Who's not ready, holler Charlie!" Voices: "One, two, three, for me!"—"Allee, allee, oxen free!"—"You're it!"—"King's X!"—"I dubs!"—"Horsler!"—"Tick-a-lock, tick-a-lock!"—"Bang, bang, you're dead!"—"Beary, Beary, off'n wood!"—"Hey, let's play Kick the Can and Call!"

He missed those sounds. Last night, lying in bed, maybe that was what he had been listening for. He hadn't been sure then; but whatever it was, it had never come. He had only heard a motorcycle going up and down the street. For years he had missed the evening sounds: Leo's mother calling her boys home for supper, the cooing of pigeons from DeLoy's barn, and the quiet swishing sounds of milking from over the fence.

The sky above was becoming overcast. Toward Red Canyon, the pink hills had taken on a bluish-gray tone; in the west there was a dun-colored haze that struck him as alien and out of place. From somewhere in the distance there came the same faint growling, grinding sound he had heard earlier, and then, louder and closer, the sudden whirring of an electric lawn mower starting up. For a moment he hesitated on the edge of the back lawn; then he stepped off, almost without thinking, and started up the street. He could see now that, at the end of town, it was the gray smoke of the sawmill that was obscuring the sky and effacing the contours of houses and trees.

He kept walking. Many of the old brick homes, he noticed, still remained; two and three stories high with ornamental gables and sometimes a cupola, they were still there even though the windows, on most of them, were boarded up, and tumbleweeds had blown against the steps and railings of the porches. But there was a naked-ness, even about those still inhabited, that bothered him. They seemed stripped, almost bleached, in fact—like a colored photo-graph carelessly overexposed. He found himself turning corners that he felt he should know; yet something was never quite right. The white picket fence was missing from in front of the tiny rock house where he had often gone to collect fast offerings or deliver a rice pudding or some raisin cookies to the little old lady everybody had called Aunt Sylvie. Gone too was the swinging gate and the arbor overhead where dark red roses and Virginia creeper had grown so heavily that the house beyond, lost in vines itself, seemed only an extension of this enchanted green cavern. Now the house stood stark and gray on a little plot of grass where a sprinkler was trying hard to rotate, but only hiccoughed in one place. And, further on, in place of the weeping willow and the coffee-colored barn where he and DeLoy had passed a summer teaching a magpie how to talk, sat a squat cinderblock house with an oversized TV antenna. From somewhere behind its aluminum door, the blare of an electric guitar sliced through the morning, and Glade hurriedly moved on.

When he passed by the school grounds, he didn't linger long. He ached to hear again the little boys' voices as they sat, legs spraddled, in the shade of the old elementary school, setting up their marbles—the steelies, aggies, taws, and migs—and singing out, "Hit'em, ya git'em, 'n' I'll lag back." But there was only the whine of an electric drill as a workman repaired something in front of the new empty school, and Glade moved on past the yellow hospital that smelled of antiseptic, the naked lawn where the old meeting-house had once stood, and finally the whitewashed Social Hall with someone's name scrawled on it with lipstick. New doors had been put on the building, and he couldn't resist trying the handle. They were locked; yet he lingered there, peering through the glass in search of something he couldn't label. Once, long ago, there had been an operetta there, and he remembered how, for weeks, he had listened to his older sisters singing, "Bread and cheese and water-cress, none can buy . . ." Did they still hold the traditional town dances—the Kris Kringle Karnival, the Mid-Winter Frolic, the '49ers, the Deer Hunter's Ball? From behind the counter where, with the Boy Scouts, he had checked coats for the crowds that came from miles around to fill the halls, he had listened longingly to the family bands tapping their feet as they played their fiddles, guitars, and accordians. Beyond these bands, though, was another one—many of the group undoubtedly dead now: he could almost hear the nasal hum of the kazoos and the rhythmic clinking of graters and eggbeaters as the ladies' Kitchen Rhythm Band tooted "Four-Leaf Clover" while the children, on Wednesday afternoons, counted out "One, two, three—back" under their breath as they jiggle-skipped, in partners, over and over, around the hall, straggling home at last with a soggy paper napkin twisted around a sticky glob of home-made fudge and a popcorn ball, a few stray pieces of hardtack and some unshelled peanuts stuck to it.

At the corner he hesitated. One or two of the old stores looked almost the same; yet so many seemed to have changed so severely that he couldn't bring himself to turn and walk down Main Street. Not yet. Just the glimpse of faded green from the corner—the town's only theater, The Gem, now obviously abandoned—caused him to turn away. Growing up without the Friday and Saturday double features seemed impossible; and life without the accompanying continued serials—would Nick Carter, the Detective, find the diamond? Could the Green Hornet get away in time?—would be little more than an endless blur of nameless days. He felt sorry for those who would never know Smiley Burnett as "Frog," or Marjorie Main as Ma Kettle, would never know Charlie McCarthy, would never hear Jeanette McDonald and Nelson Eddy sing, would never see *Smiling Through* or *Blossoms in the Dust*, or stop each time they hear the theme from Tchaikovsky's Fifth Symphony, recalling the weekly documentary and its closing words, "Time marches on . . ."

A car came by, and the woman driver stared at him but he decided it was someone he didn't know. He crossed the street, still moving west. On the corner, more than thirty-five summers ago, an itinerant Italian fruit peddler had stationed his cart full of oranges and bananas, calling through the green afternoon his corrupted version of "This way! This way!" sounding more to children's ears like "Dishwater! Dishwater!" A few dandelions still grew by the ditchbank, but the ditch itself was empty now. Did anyone still race popsicle-stick boats from one end of the town to the other? Did they still occasionally "borrow" a watermelon from the P.I.E. truck parked on the corner on summer nights? Were they still making chocolate peanut butter fudge that sometimes went to sugar or went hard in the pan on the back porch while you tried to beat it after it cooled? And on the Saturday before Easter, did they still go "Easter-ing" in hordes to Red Canyon, baskets packed with salads and sandwiches—and plenty of hardboiled eggs to roll down the pink hillside? Were they still soaping windows on Halloween and kicking valentines on Valentine's Day?

The growling noise he had heard earlier seemed louder, steadier now, and he could see that, beyond the small hill at the end of the street where the Forest Service Headquarters still stood, the air was heavy with dark smoke. He moved on, noticing the street signs and sidewalks that had not been there when he was a boy. Many of the houses, it occurred to him, were now numbered with metallic digits. As elsewhere, the picket fences had been removed, and the trees and vines were gone. Somewhere along this street, he remembered, there had been a sort of cottage where the whole front yard had been a dense flower garden. It had always reminded him of the painting hanging on the wall in the dining room above the big brown radio. He kept thinking, as he walked, that he would surely find the house —or the spot where it had been—in this block, or the next, but when he neared the place where the street finally crossed the river and came to an end before the Forest Service entrance, he felt confused, wondering how he had missed it or if maybe it had never been there at all.

Not being able to find the house unsettled him; but what disturbed him more now was the dry riverbed under the new bridge, the trailers parked off to the right, and the flat vacant lots that stretched away on both sides of him. The trees! This had been a forest where hundreds of birds flitted among the leaves and the river gushed coolly over the smooth stones.

The grinding, snarling noise was much louder now, and through the sparse trees at the end of the barren lot across the road he could see, rising above the parked cars and trucks, the coneshaped burners of the sawmill. He looked behind him. In the quiet of summer afternoons he had slipped down into the green woods, followed the stream as it wound along, stopping now and then to dip a strainer, borrowed from the kitchen, down into the clear water where it lingered in still, shallow pools along the river's edge, gathering up dozens of tiny minnows.

Across the road the woods had been thick too, and he moved there now, having to slip between two strands of barbed wire before he stood on the flat lot where the towering cottonwoods had been. The smoke from the sawmill was thicker here. He hesitated, then walked into it, as if moving through a fog.

The Airdome was gone. Set back among the trees and elevated on blocks, the large wooden structure had been sheltered by a massive roof yet left open at the sides. Long after it had fallen into disuse, it had been visited on summer afternoons by boys who climbed its rafters, roller-skated across its wooden floor, or pondered the mysteries of the adult world in the coolness of its sun-dappled shade. And before that—Glade winced now, becoming intensely aware of his hunger, aware that he had wandered all the way here without having eaten anything. But what had he been thinking of? Oh yes, the Airdome. The Airdome before, the Airdome as it had been even earlier than those lazy summer days when, no longer a child and not yet a teenager, he had explored its neglected cavernous interior. Long ago, before that, it had been almost a symbol of that other, more grown-up world, a reminder of what was ahead, of what was waiting somewhere out there beyond the grass-stained knees and minnows in Mason jars and "Kick the Can and Call!" On warm summer nights, sleeping out of doors, he had lain awake smelling the green grass and listening to the faraway, steady beat of the bass drum coming from the Airdome. Once he had walked in the dark, following the gurgling water in the ditch, up past Main Street, past the little cottage with the garden, until he came to the bridge, the water running swiftly beneath him, watching the lights flickering through the trees and hearing the swishes and shuffles of the grown-ups as they danced and shouted, while the open-air dance hall vibrated to the thump-and-twang songs whose actual names he had not learned until years later, names like "Red Wing" and "Cherokee." But that was the last year they ever held the summer dances at the Airdome.

He moved in and out of the smoke, feeling driven by an ache different from hunger now, crossing still another barbed-wire fence until he was standing beside a pile of scraps and sawdust, watching the flames leap from the smoky openings in the huge burners while the grinding rattle of the saws and planes rang and grated in his ears. One of the workers noticed him and seemed to wave a gloved hand at him before disappearing inside a corrugated aluminum shed, but Glade was sure he didn't know him. At the foot of one of the burners, an old man and a little boy stacked scraps of lumber into a gray-green pickup.

It was late, he realized. He thought of the boys and Shelley, awake now and wondering where he had gone; and he pictured Bernice trying to keep them from going out until he was home to supervise them. The scraps. They would like them, it occurred to him—something to play with. All of them were builders—the boys especially, unlike him, were always obsessed with constructing cities, machines, anything. He stooped down and picked up a block of wood, trying to think, despite the overpowering noise. He would have to come back later with the station wagon. He glanced up at the burners, heard the large rotating chains rattling as they ascended shakily up the ramp, carrying on them the quivering remaining ends of the sawed boards and dropping them off into the dark opening near the top of the burner. He wasn't sure he liked the idea of bringing the kids up here, though.

Homecoming

The old man was looking at him with a smile strangely familiar, while he seemed to be motioning with the back of his hand for him to go ahead and pick up any scraps he wanted. Glade hesitated. Although he really couldn't place who he was, it was as though the old man was someone he should have known. The boy too was disconcertingly familiar. Glade felt his stomach tighten, and he ached to go back in time to see it all played back to him now like an endless home movie.

He glanced now at the platform at the foot of the burner where, a few minutes before, the man and the boy had been removing the blocks of wood before the vibrating track carried the pieces up and dumped them inside the burner. Maybe if he hurried, he could gather up a few scraps now and catch a ride home with the old man. Suddenly the growl of the planer seemed to grow louder, and the heat from the burners became oppressive. Seeing that the old man and the boy were still fidgeting with their load of scraps in the back of the pickup, Glade suddenly leaped up on the platform and began gathering up the first few blocks of wood as they jiggled up the bulky rattling chains.

He didn't see it happen, but the instant he felt his arm wrenched roughly against the rotating track and then, in horror, saw himself being yanked from the platform and pulled, beyond his control, onto the vibrating chain ascending into the burner, he screamed out as loudly as he could and tried with all his strength to tear his arm from the sleeve caught in the chain. But the roar grew louder until even he couldn't hear his own voice, and as he tore frantically at the jacket sleeve, he threw his head back, imagining for an instant he saw the pickup, blurred and far below him now, driving away in the dust.

The Reunion

Well, if you'd of been in my shoes, do you suppose you'd of done any different? I doubt it. I don't care what they say, there's only so much they can expect a person to have to put up with. And I'm not one to bellyache, believe you me. I wouldn't even try to tell you what I've been put through over the last ten or twelve years: why, one time during the bottling season I was so laid up with arthritis, not to mention a leg all swoll up like a balloon and a bad ear on top of that, that I can tell you I thought for sure they was just going to have to put me away like that old dog of Parley J.'s that got hit by the dump truck.

But anyway, as I was trying to say, they can only expect a person to take just so much. Now they can say all they want about putting on the dog and turning the other cheek, but if they'd of had to put up with a tenth of what I've had to put up with, believe you me, it would of been a whole different story. The thing of it was, they never should of announced on the radio that the flood was off. Oh, it was off all right—at least it never came, or anyway what little bit finally did come piddling down the ditch never amounted to anything. But if they just hadn't of announced it ahead of time I never would of gone. I would of been here taking care of the garden and checking the basement and probably none of this would of happened. At least it could of happened without me.

Well, anyhow, what finally come about never should of come about at all. I never planned to go in the first place, what with the flood scare and all and then them raising the water level on top of that. Oh, I might of said something to Neldean and Millard when they was up last spring, but I'll tell you this summer did me right in, what with all the apricots I tried to put up and all the time I had to

130

spend in that garden with it as hot as it was and not a drop of rain all summer long. I was so give out come the end of August that I wasn't about to go anywhere, Griffin Reunion or not. But then all that rain hit us, and just when I thought it was never going to let up and they was saying every day how close we was to having the first September flood in the history of Utah County, then all of a sudden it stopped and they said the flood was called off and the next thing I knew here was JaeNell and all of them asking why in the dickens I never told them I wasn't coming when they were all going to a lot of bother to combine the whole affair with Thurza's ninetieth birthday and who knows what all.

Well, needless to say, I went. And you can bet it'll be a darn long time before they ever get me to another one of those things, even if they said they was going to hold it right here in Santaquin. Anyway, I got me a ride and went up there because Leola insisted on making such a big to-do about it all and then was afraid that nobody was going to come. Well, they come all right, and it would of been a darn sight better if half of them had stayed home. The first thing she did was palm us off on every cat and dog in Tooele. She had the whole thing arranged, me staying at JaeNell's, Neldean and Millard over at LuGene and Carvel's, Wren and Creta stuck off somewhere clear to the other end of town with some stray relative of Elwood's that nobody'd ever heard of. Wyoma was the smart one. (All three of them was there—Wyoma, Utahna, and Uvada—the first time I'd seen any one of those girls since Osmer died.) Well, Utahna and Uvada, see, drove down together from Ogden and had to get right back to their husbands, who was the only ones as far as I could tell that had the good sense not to come. But Wyoma, the younger one, come in on the plane, all the way from California, and she was not about to turn around and go right back any more than she was about to let Leola fix her up at somebody's house she'd never heard tell of. When she come in from Salt Lake on the bus, she had DeVor pick her up right there at the bus station or wherever it was and take her straight to his home. Well, if you don't think that didn't cause an uproar—DeVor's wife dead no more than six months and just him and those three rattle-headed kids of his alone in the house! I thought we'd never hear the end of it. Leola told everybody how DeVor was supposed to of had the Jolleys staying at his place and how she and Elwood could of made arrangements to put Wyoma up at their place if she'd even had the courtesy to write and say she was about to come. Well, Wyoma let it be known loud and clear that the main reason she even come at all was to see DeVor. She said she'd always been close to Doreen and DeVor, and if she was going to come to Tooele at all then there simply wasn't any question but that she'd stay at her own cousin-in-law's. Well, Leola was quick to remind everybody that DeVor and Wyoma had been beaus long before he ever ended up marrying Doreen, and it sure seemed funny to her that Wyoma had never been interested enough in her cousin as to fly all the way out here *before* she died. And what Leola wanted to know was what was poor Chuck thinking about all this all the way down there in Yuba City.

But that was Leola. Myself, I kind of sided with Wyoma—at least at first. But you should of seen the heads turn when she come walking in that kitchen there, all gussied up, plucked eyebrows and all, nibbling at the olives and bread-and-butter pickles, and telling everybody how much she loved every one of them. There was Utahna and Uvada, both of them big as a barn, looking like they wanted to drop right through the floor. And to make matters worse, one of Neldean's girls had the nerve to ask right out so everybody could hear which one of them was Wyoma's mother, Utahna or Uvada! But anyway, as I said, Wyoma might of been a fool to push herself off onto DeVor, but at least she made up her mind where she was going to stay and stuck to it, no two ways about it. The rest of us—ha! You should of seen the three-ring circus.

You see, the Reunion was originally set up for Saturday, and even though Thurza's ninetieth birthday was actually not until Tuesday, they got it in their heads they'd try to celebrate it Saturday so everybody'd get a piece of the cake. But then Darrel D. writes a card from Amarillo, Texas, saying he's on his way home for his grandma's party and can't get in until Sunday night, so the next thing you know they're turning everything around and putting the party on Monday, which is Labor Day, and keeping the Reunion on Saturday in case some of them can't stay over, and mixing everybody up until none of us knew what was what. Julene was the one that was put out. Here she come driving all the way up from Soldier Summit, bringing her eighty-six-year-old mother-in-law who has no control over her bowels but still insisted on coming to see Thurza on her birthday, and when they got here, they no sooner got out of the car than here come Leola and them telling them the party wasn't till Monday and could they possibly drive back up again then. Well, Julene really kicked up a stink wanting to know why nobody'd told them, and here was Leola trying to think up some way to have some of Elwood's folks put them up for the whole weekend, loose bowels and all, and if you don't think that didn't cause a hubbub! And then, to top it all off, here, about noon, Burns and Hazel come driving up with a car clear full of the noisiest kids you ever saw, and before anybody'd got two words out, here's Burns telling everybody how hurt VerDee was that nobody ever thought to invite them and Leola telling everybody that she knows darn well and good that if they were on the list, they got an invitation like everyone else, and Burns saying, well, that might be, but according to VerDee this makes three reunions in a row that they've been ignored and, although Burns claims VerDee never said it, Burns thinks VerDee feels that it's all on account of Nida being part Eskimo and always getting left out of everything.

Well, instead of having the Reunion in some nice park, Leola had got it in her head at the last minute that she wanted to hold it in her backyard. LuGene and Carvel said if it was going to be held in anybody's backyard, it ought to be in theirs, as theirs was sure a darn sight bigger and didn't have all that broken lawn furniture stacked up on the patio to boot. But Leola, I guess, wanted to show off her new indoor-outdoor carpet in her kitchen, and besides that, the day before the Reunion, LuGene and Carvel had cut a big hole in their living room wall, as LuGene had been telling Carvel she was sure she'd been hearing a buzzing sound for over a month and Carvel thought she was crazy as a loon until she made him knock a hole in the wall and they found a six-foot honeycomb and more bees than you can shake a stick at. Well, the next thing you knew, LuGene and Carvel was driven right out of house and home and had to stay over at Carvel's folks' place while the termite-people tried to scare all of those bees out of there, and when Neldean and Millard arrived and found out what had happened, Millard was so put out, he took Neldean and got them a motel and don't think we won't hear about *that* for the next ten years.

Anyway, here Leola thought everyone was coming to her house, and at two-thirty LuGene and Carvel still hadn't showed up and JaeNell told her it was probably because they were hurt that it wasn't going to be at their house, bees or not, and Utahna was all upset that nobody'd seen hide nor hair of Dexter and Veloy when she knew darn well that they was supposed to be bringing Aunt Essie Proctor and a whole bunch of other people and, last she had heard, was planning on leaving Kaysville about the same time she and Uvada drove down from Ogden. Well, this upset Leola no end, and in all the hubbub, Thurza wandered out and got in some stray car (she's always saying how Nettie's coming to get her) and nobody could find her for twenty minutes, and after that got settled down, Leola made Elwood go to the store and buy about twenty of those little cartons of potato salad as Dexter and Veloy was supposed to be bringing it and here it was almost three o'clock and no potato salad or Veloy or Aunt Essie Proctor or any of the others they was supposed to have with them. Well, what happened was this: no sooner had Elwood loaded up his car with potato salad at the store, than he decided he'd just drive by the park, and when he got there, there was Dexter and Veloy and two other cars full of people that'd been waiting there at the Pavilion since one-thirty. Well, Dexter was so mad that nobody'd told him the place had been changed, and Veloy was upset with Dexter for not driving down to Leola's and checking instead of just sitting there for an hour and a half, and she was put out with Elwood for buying all that potato salad for fear how nobody'd eat hers, and Elwood wouldn't speak to Leola for not putting up a sign at the park telling that the place had been changed, and JaeNell was so mad at both her ma and her dad that she gathered up her kids and went home, and it took Creta and Utahna both to go down and get her to come back as she was in charge of the Sing-Along and nobody else knew all the tunes.

Well, the afternoon wasn't so bad, considering what was to come later. Wyoma insisted on dishing up DeVor's dessert for him, which didn't set too well with some of the folk there, Julene had to keep taking her mother-in-law to the bathroom, and Thurza kept getting up every few minutes while they was trying to elect next year's president, telling everybody that she'd better go wait on the curb as Nettie was coming after her. And wouldn't you know that with all that potato salad—five times more than you could eat in a week—there wasn't a drop of anything to drink, since whoever it was on the punch committee never showed up, and Leola and JaeNell had to run in and concoct something out of cream of tartar and colored water. But, as I say, things got a darn sight worse as time went on.

You'd of thought that everybody'd be so wore out by then they would of just gone home and gone to bed and not give a hoot whether they came back to Thurza's party or not. Well, those that had good sense did. And I would of too if I hadn't of thought that somebody ought to be there to represent Santaquin. They don't need to think that Tooele is the only place on the map. Well, anyway, when it come time for everybody to kiss and hug and shake hands and talk about what a good time they'd had, I couldn't find hide nor hair of JaeNell. Uvada told me that Lance had come and gathered up her and the kids and took them home without saying a word, but Creta said that her car was still parked across the street. Somebody said they thought they'd gone off in the pickup to Coronet's to get Becky Sue some school shoes before the stores closed, but here I was as wore out as I could be, and LuGene and Carvel begging me to go down and stay with them and their herd of bees. LuGene had made this big pot of corned beef and cabbage and froze it, thinking she was going to have a house full of company, and now it looked like they wasn't going to have a soul, as Neldean and Millard had already paid for a motel clear off somewhere on the other side of town. Well, I thought the least I could do is visit with them while they give me a ride out to JaeNell's, but when we got there you wouldn't of believed the mess.

The house was wide open and you'd of thought a whirlwind must of hit it. First of all, they live way out there in the toolies without a speck of grass planted yet, and you had to climb over all the tricycles and roller skates to even get up on the porch and then wade through a pile of doll buggies and wet bathing suits before you could get through the front door. Well, I was sure somebody'd come in there and kidnapped the whole lot of them and then beat it with my overnight bag (you see, JaeNell had took it from me that morning thinking I was going to be staying with them), but LuGene come in behind me and set me straight on that, telling me that was just the way JaeNell keeps house. She never was much for house-work, LuGene says, and now that Lance has been laid off work it's just gone from bad to worse. But anyway, what I was concerned about was what in the world had she done with my overnight bag. We went through that house of hers from top to bottom and when we come to that bathroom sink full of baby didies I told LuGene, come on, we're not staying here another minute. Well, wouldn't you know that we no sooner marched out of there than here come Leola driving up in the truck, followed by Julene and that old Mrs. Twitchell or whatever her name is, and here she was bringing *them* down there to stay as well. Well, I wasn't about to stay for love nor money *then*—what with a messy kitchen, a sink full of them stinky didies, and Julene's poor old mother-in-law to boot. And you can bet you wouldn't of been able to find an Air Wick in the place.

Anyway, LuGene and me piled back in the car and Carvel drove us off to Coronet's to look for JaeNell and Lance and find out what in the world they done with my overnight bag. Well, that was a wild goose chase if I ever seen one. There was Burns and Hazel just going in the minute we drove up, so they said they'd help us keep an eye peeled for JaeNell or any of them. Me and LuGene went off down one side of the store where they keep their shoes, and Carvel took off after Burns and Hazel down the other. Now, they didn't say a word about where we was to meet and here in a minute we run into Lance and the boys, but couldn't find the rest of them, so we all went off looking for JaeNell and trying to keep an eye out for Carvel. Well, if you'd of seen the people in that store you'd of known it was Labor Day weekend and no question about it. It was all me and LuGene could do to keep track of each other, let alone try to herd Lance and those three nincompoops of his. Well, after going up and down those aisles, here comes Burns telling us Hazel had found JaeNell for us and they'd gone up one side looking for us while Carvel went off to see if we was down by draperies and hard-ware. We sent Lance and the boys to stand guard at the door and look for any of them, while me and LuGene went down through the middle. I'll tell you we hunted that darn store down until we was both blue in the face and finally plowed our way back to the door all give out to find out that Burns had got hold of Hazel and JaeNell but they'd just gone off again to see if *we* was lost. Finally here come

JaeNell (who said, by the way, that my overnight bag was still up at her mother's where she left it), so LuGene went off to hunt up Carvel and tell him we'd finally found her, and when he finally showed up all riled up because he'd been waiting for us for twenty minutes over by the shoes, then I had to go round up LuGene and tell her we'd found Carvel. Well, if the Reunion didn't wear us out, that did. I told JaeNell I didn't want to put her out, what with Julene and her mother-in-law going to be there and LuGene and Carvel feeling all left out that there wasn't going to be a soul up at their place. So, Carvel took me by Leola's where things was still helter-skelter, and we finally hunted down my overnight bag where some-body'd stuck it inside the hall closet and then headed off up to LuGene and Carvel's.

Well, to make a long story short, when we got there, there was a whole carload of people, Aunt Essie Proctor and all of them, that Leola had sent up there so LuGene and Carvel wouldn't be without anybody. If you don't think I wasn't ready to turn around and leave! If I'd of known where Neldean and Millard's motel was, I would of high-tailed it up there and told them to move over. Well, as it happened, I spotted Thurza sitting out front in somebody's car and I just gathered up my bag and went over and got in with her. After all, it was her birthday they'd talked me into staying for any-way. She, of course, thought I was Nettie half the time and had come to get her. Well, come to find out that the people Thurza lives with are just a house or two away from LuGene and Carvel's and, in a few minutes, here they come to get her and you wouldn't of believed how tickled they was to see she had company. Of course, they begged me to stay the night and, believe you me, they didn't have to beg too long, as I was so give out I would of slept in the street. And almost had to.

Well, here I was in Tooele at the Griffin Reunion, and staying with folks I'd never laid eyes on in my whole life. But at least it wasn't any of that tribe on Elwood's side of the family. Who it was, come to find out, was the Esplins—Pratt and Zarahemla—both in their eighties, I suspect, and no relation whatsoever to us, but second cousin to Thurza on her mother's side. Now I'm not saying they was outright odd, but then they wasn't any of your run-of-the-mill everyday folks either—not by a long shot. Creta tried to tell me later that Leola had told her they was related some way to that polygamist outfit down in Short Creek, but all I got from them is that they was healers of some sort and had had the law after them a time or two. They believe in keeping fit, and what two tablespoons of vinegar in a glass of hot water three times a day won't do, a heaping spoonful of cayenne pepper will. Zarahemla, she fixed us all a bit of supper, and it was old Brother Esplin's job to test it all out with the solar bob. They keep it hanging right there in the kitchen by the ironing board, and before he'd let any of us eat a bite, he had to swing this thing over our food to make sure it was fit to eat. Well, according to the solar bob, it was pure enough, so we ate our sprouts and millet cakes, and when poor Thurza fell asleep and keeled off her chair, we decided we'd all had a big enough day. And, believe you me, it didn't take any hot water and vinegar to make *me* sleep like a log.

Now Sunday, they said, was supposed to be a good day, but you can bet if they can think up some way to switch it on you, they'll do it. Well, we had thunder showers and hail and the wind blowing to beat the band and I don't know what all else, but I do know that they had me running every which way from the time I got up until the time I went to bed. LuGene and Carvel sent Ruthie Ann over before any of us was hardly up, to tell me to be sure and go to their ward to Sunday School because she was going to be giving the sacrament gem and Carvel himself was conducting the meeting. We no sooner sat down to a cup of postum and was testing it out by the solar bob than here comes the biggest kid of JaeNell's huffing and puffing up there on his bicycle to tell me they was coming to pick me up in half an hour to go to their ward because his ma wanted me to see his brother get to pass the sacrament. And I'd hardly got into my dress and got some lipstick on, when here come Leola honking outside, the car filled to the top with Neldean and Millard and Wren and Creta and half a dozen others, and come to find out, she'd gathered us all up and carted us off to *her* ward to watch *her* lead the choir.

Well, thank the Lord it turned out to be Fast Sunday and *every-body* just stayed on there to Testimony Meeting or else we'd of had to go through the whole rigamarole again that afternoon, deciding who was going where to watch who do what. What burned LuGene up (and JaeNell too, I found out later) was that they could of took me to either one of their wards for Sunday School and I still could of gone at noon to Leola's Testimony Meeting to hear the choir sing their special number. But it was bad enough the way it was, being dragged here and then dragged there until I didn't know which way was up. LuGene was hurt that I'd stayed at Esplins and then gone off with Leola and Elwood, and JaeNell was really put out that I hadn't stayed with her and, what's more, wasn't even there when she come all the way up there to get me for Sunday School after she'd sent that kid of hers clear across town to give me the message and all. Anyway, who was going to eat where turned out to be another ordeal and I won't bother to go into *that*. Just take my word for it that me and Neldean and Millard got us some Chinese food at the Center Cafe. And at suppertime I had warmed-up corned beef and cabbage with LuGene and Carvel and listened while they carried on about Leola and gave me all the dirt on Wyoma and DeVor, and then I cut through the block and had strawberries and ice cream over at DeVor's while they had a few things to say about LuGene and Carvel and a couple of things on Millard that I wouldn't want to repeat too loud. Anyway, I was glad to get back to the Esplins and Thurza and let my ear cool off—although I'd of given anything to of been able to tune in to what was being broadcast over at Leola's or out at JaeNell's—to say nothing of the little chit-chat I understand Wren and Creta and Millard and Neldean had cooked up out at the White City Motel.

When Monday come, I felt like I'd been away for a month, and I was ready to catch the first ride going anywhere within forty miles of Santaquin—which I should have done, too, but there was Darrel D. bright and early, home from Amarillo and sleeping on Esplin's sofa when I got up. Now I suppose you've got to give him credit for coming all the way back to Utah just for a bite of cake—after all, he's just about all Thurza's really got in the world since she never had kids of her own except, I guess, Garland, Darrel D.'s dad, who she raised single-handed after his own dad got tromped by a horse—but what I want to know is, why in the world did Darrel D. think he had to come bringing that galoot of a kid from Tallahassee with him? I heard all the hubbub in the night and I should of known then they was going to throw a monkey-wrench into the whole mess. Well, Sister Esplin evidently got up in the middle of the night and let Darrel D. and this Boone kid in, but why she didn't just let him take a blanket and curl up on the floor to the side of Darrel D. is beyond me. But she didn't do that. Instead, she told Darrel D. he could sleep on the sofa but his friend would have to go next door and sleep at LuGene's as they've got that new addition they've built on and all. I don't suppose she mentioned as well that they also had a six-foot hornet's nest and a whole carload of people from up north strung out all over creation. Well, why Darrel D. didn't notice all those cars in the driveway is beyond me, but evidently when he got Carvel up in the middle of the night and tried to push this strange kid that nobody knew from Adam off on him and LuGene, Carvel just asked him what he thought this was, a hotel or what, and sent him hotfooting it straight over to DeVor's. Now JaeNell thinks he done that deliberately just to spite DeVor, but LuGene claims he done it to make things look respectable, as DeVor and Wyoma should of had a chaperone over there right from the start, those kids of his being altogether too young and too scatterbrained to know beans about what might or might not be going on right under their own roof.

Well, it would of been bad enough without that. All we needed was another bunch of people to add to the confusion, and here about ten o'clock in the morning come Newell and Darlene up from Oakley. Now Newell was Garland's half brother, which makes him some sort of half-uncle to Darrel D. and I don't know what to Thurza—but Newell had a different ma than Garland (in fact, she and Newell's dad were own cousins and that might explain why some of the kids never seemed quite right). Anyway, here comes Newell and Darlene bringing their two teenaged girls, Darla and Twila, who insisted on turning cartwheels and doing the splits all morning out on LuGene's lawn and making Carvel ready to tear out his hair, afraid they were going to trample all over his new little tams he'd just planted. And those girls, they wouldn't sit still a minute; you'd of thought they both had Saint Vitus's dance. But then their mother was a lot like that (don't ask me why she married Newell), and these girls was both just about as talented and double-jointed as Darlene herself used to be (I'll never forget how she could almost stick her tongue right up her nose) but with both Esplins' and LuGene's places in such a muddle, I told them they ought to go over in that big backyard of DeVor's to practice their cheerleading. Well, I'll come back to that later, but the next thing I knew, here come Newell and Darlene in the house carrying this huge cake they'd had in the trunk of the car and, if you ask me, was smelling to high heaven like gasoline. LuGene stepped right in and told her she'd help her fix up the part of the decorations that had started to droop, and in a minute there was Darlene in the bedroom crying to beat the band because she had decorated the thing herself and now LuGene was making her feel like it was all sagging and lopsided, which, if you want to know the honest truth, it *was*. But that was only the beginning, because Leola called up LuGene to ask her if anybody knew for sure what time they were supposed to gather at her house for the party, and LuGene set her straight right then that, since the Reunion had been at Leola's, the birthday party should be at *their* place. Outside, Sister Esplin was pacing up and down the sidewalk telling everybody that Thurza had just set herself down in her rocker and told everybody loud and clear that she was too give out to go anywhere, and when LuGene and Leola had finally had it out and Leola had give in to let her go ahead and have the big to-do at her place, here come JaeNell and Julene and that little Twitchell lady driving up with two big sheets of bakery cake that Leola'd ordered for the party—and if you don't think that didn't set Darlene off bawling again in the back bedroom!

Well, this made Newell's blood rise and so Veloy ran and got Dexter to take Newell off for a little walk to cool him off, and, to top it all off, they ended up over at DeVor's house where Darla and Twila was falling all over this Boone kid from Tallahassee. Now I suspect this was nowhere near the first time Newell had seen those girls of his all googly-eyed over some guy, but what riled him up right away was the fact that this galoot was out there trying to sell them a big fat Bible and it looked to Newell for all the world like he was trying to convert them. Evidently that's what Darrel D. has been doing back there in Amarillo—selling Bibles with this guy and a bunch of others. But Darrel D. apparently had the good sense to not try to play the big salesman around his own folks—at least he hadn't yet—whereas this Boone galoot must of started in the minute he got over there with Wyoma and DeVor, because here come

Wyoma out of the back door waving her new Bible and trying to tell Newell, who's her own second cousin, to calm down. Well, this got Newell's goat, as he could see right away that this friend of Darrel D.'s had really made an impression on Wyoma already and, for all he knew, had not only sold her a Bible but had sold her a big hunk of his pentecostal religion and those big blue eyes of his as well. Here I was, trying to watch all of this over the back fence, and here was Darla and Twila pulling at their dad, who always was a hot-head, and him trying to get at this Boone kid who said something that really made him boil, and then all of a sudden there was Wyoma getting in there between them and trying to save this galoot, when DeVor stepped out on the back porch and jerked Wyoma out of the way and hauled off and hit this Boone kid such a good one that it sent him reeling off into the turnips and this big Bible of his that must of weighed a good five pounds flew up and hit me right square in the eye where you see this scar here by my eyebrow.

Oh, I was so mad I couldn't see straight. Dexter come and rescued me out of the garden I was staggering around in, and I could hear Wyoma bawling over there and trailing off after DeVor, while Newell yanked those blubbering girls through the fence and stuck them in the back of the car and then sat there honking and yelling at Darlene. Leola and JaeNell were running all over trying to find Thurza who'd disappeared, and come to find out she was halfway down the block trailing after this bloody-nosed Boone kid who she thought was one of Nettie's boys come to get her. Darrel D. went off and finally got them back, but that was the end of the party right there, which, I guess, didn't matter a whole lot as Wren and Creta had just drove up while all this was going on and announced that, according to what they'd just discovered in Creta's Book of Remembrance, it wasn't even Thurza's ninetieth birthday anyway, but only her eighty-ninth.

That was all I could take. I stood there holding an ice cube on my right eye and telling them right and left exactly what I thought about their reunions and birthday parties and everything else. JaeNell had the nerve to come and try to shush me and I told her to go home and get them didies out of the sink and into the wash before she tried to set *me* straight. Oh, was I mad. Parley J. and Norma Jean both says they're afraid it's going to be a long time before I ever see another invitation to a reunion and I told them both it'd be a darn cold day before they'd ever catch me at another one either. And I told them, just like I'm telling you, I could of handled a whole flood a darn sight easier than that weekend up there. It makes you wish they hadn't of called it off after all but just gone ahead and had it.

Souvenir

The words, by now, had almost lost their meaning: his mind still said them, and sometimes he could even hear them struggling painfully up through his throat—"Don't let her die, don't let her die"—but most of all they had become a sort of numbing chant that helped to shut out the world barreling noisily on, irreverently and incongruously, while she lay up there clutching the white sheet and praying, he suspected, to be allowed to go.

The whole thing, to Cary, seemed wrong: the leaves turning yellow too early, then the weather becoming suddenly and unseasonably hot, and now the too-happy sounds of children as they threw bread crumbs to the ducks and splashed in the water along the edge of the lake. He wanted to stop them, ask them if they realized what they were doing, yet he knew it was no concern of theirs, that they were innocently ignorant, wholly oblivious to the fact that, beyond the trees of Liberty Park, beyond the noisy traffic of downtown, up on the Avenues in a quiet hospital room, a thirty-seven-year-old woman was dying of cancer.

Even the word *woman*, as he thought it to himself, was not right. She was still just a girl and, in a way, scarcely different from their daughter, now eighteen, who would be starting her first year at the university in another week. Yet that was really a lie too, and he knew it the moment he thought it, because Veda hardly even resembled herself anymore, let alone reflected Libby or any other young girl just out of high school.

He didn't like to think of her thinness, of the way her eyes, day by day, seemed to sink back in the hollow grayness under her bony brow, and he tried to fix his attention now on anything else, on the way the bark had evidently been gouged on the trunk of a tree and

144

now seemed to be healing over, or the way a particular leaf, the sun coming through it now from the other side, acquired an almost startling luminosity. But he found it difficult to keep his mind on anything for very long. Within seconds almost he would feel the impatience rising up within him, and the recurring thought that time was running out and that, if he could only think, there might still be avenues untried, some hope yet unexplored. But he remembered again the feeling he had had—a tinge of surprise followed by the shiver of recognition—when, years ago, he had read that the Kennedy infant had died, or that, much more recently, doctors had been unable to save Onassis. Surely, he had thought, surely there were doctors somewhere, the best surgeons, the top medical specialists, that could be summoned, flown in from New York or Stockholm or Geneva, if only expense were no obstacle. It had been hard for him, as a boy, to think that even the famous and the wealthy were not immune to the mundane humilities of measles and mumps, that there was not some magic talisman out there somewhere that could protect one against anything if only the check were large enough or carried the proper signature: even now he found it difficult to give up the idea that, if only he could read the right things or query the right people, the possibility of hope was still there and death was not inevitable.

"All we can do now is pray," Veda's mother had said, months ago. And there were times when he was certain the praying had helped. The last time he had laid his hands on her dark hair and asked, once again, that she might be made well, he had honestly felt, despite a twinge of selfishness, that the prayer had been heard. But something frightening was happening now, something he didn't like to think about. Only two days ago, just as he had kissed Veda's cheek and started to leave the bedside, she had reached out for his hand and clung to it, pleading, as much with her eyes as with her voice, from behind a pained smile: "Cary—please let me go."

He shifted his weight uneasily now and looked around him. A father was lifting his little boy up to the drinking fountain; two other boys ducked behind trees, firing imaginary guns, then scampered off in the direction of the aviary. Maybe Libby would be back already. It was still more than forty-five minutes earlier than she had said, and yet he was tired of trying to think of what to do with the rest of the time. He looked off through the trees. There was something restful, even soothing, about Liberty Park—especially at this time of year. Even here it was hard to keep his mind from drifting up the Avenues to the figure breathing quietly against the sheets in the small white room, yet it was easier than sitting alone in the empty house, walking from room to room, listening always for some unknown sound but hearing only the steady ticking of the clock. Looking through the boxes of things he had saved for Libby had somewhat eased the morning hours, but after spending half of the afternoon at the hospital ("Go home, Cary," Veda's mother had said, "and try to get some rest"), he couldn't face going back to the house just yet and had turned off 7th East and driven into the park.

It was surprising, almost shocking, it occurred to him, how long it had been since the last time he had come here. In those days before Saltair had burned down and the Rainbow Rendezvous metamorphosed into the Terrace, he and Veda had inevitably driven home by way of the park on warm summer nights, taking time to walk by the lake and the sleeping merry-go-round. And up until Libby had been ten or twelve, he had brought her here on special "Daddy-Daughter Dates," letting her choose cotton candy or a snow cone, and leaving it up to her whether they rowed around the lake or visited the monkeys and the birds. Today too, he suddenly realized, was going to be a sort of Daddy-Daughter Date—their first in a long, long time. He looked at his watch and grew impatient: almost as though they were his own momentoes, his own memories, he could feel himself becoming excited about the boxes he had taken down from the hall closet. He glanced once more at his watch, thought again of Veda with a little twinge of pain, then decided to walk quickly through the aviary and then drive home, even if it would still be a little early.

When he arrived at the house, Libby was already home, standing in the kitchen in her cut-off Levis making a peanut-butter sandwich. "Hi, Daddy," he heard her mumble through the rooms. Then: "How was Mom?"

"About the same."

"I want to go see her tonight," she said, coming to the doorway of the living room and resting against the door frame. "But I'll have to go in *my* car because I've got to drop some things off at Julie's and then afterwards I'm going to go meet Cindy and those guys at Trolley Square."

It was still hard for him to believe how grown-up she was: even in the Levis, with her dark hair hanging straight, she was a young lady instead of a little girl.

"Do you want me to come back and fix you something?" she asked, looking as if she were trying to read his gaze.

"No, no," he assured her. "I'll grab something up there."

He glanced off through the doorway to the boxes visible just inside the hall. He wanted it to be something special; it was hard, though, to know how to start it. She must have followed his glance for, immediately, he heard her voice: "Hey, what's with all this stuff in the hall, anyway? Is it going to Deseret Industries or something?"

It was started. He hurried to the hall and began carrying the boxes, two and three at a time, into the front room. "Did you see what was in them?"

"Yah—a lot of it's my old stuff." She sounded puzzled.

"All of it's yours. We saved it for you." He brought in the last two boxes and put them with the others in the center of the living room, and then sat down on the carpet, his back against the couch. He felt excited, yet, because of something in her voice, he also felt a tinge of uneasiness.

"When was the last time you looked at any of this?" he asked, opening one of the boxes and taking out a paint-spattered set of watercolors, a bent pencil box, and a thick stack of coloring books.

"Gosh, I don't know—last year maybe. Why?"

Last year. That seemed impossible.

"I mean, Mom used to get them down from time to time. And if I ever needed anything—"

He set the coloring books aside and tried another box. There were books and toys he longed to see and touch again that he knew were not among these: the Clippo the Clown puppet, the Daniel Boone coonskin cap, the fragile records of *Gulliver's Travels*, the book of *Little Black Sambo*. He pulled up the cardboard flaps. There were dolls and some stuffed animals inside.

"Remember Anna Livia Plurabelle?" He held up a wilted and almost faceless Raggedy Ann. "We named her after something we read in college. Henry James or James Joyce or one of those. You used to love her."

"I still do," Libby said, taking the doll and turning it over slowly. "She's awfully ratty, though." She put her down.

"How about Brahmsy?" He held up a brown bear, a large key protruding from its back where much of the imitation fur had worn away. "It used to play 'Brahms' *Lullaby*,' remember?" He tried to twist the key but it wouldn't turn.

"I got that out two or three times to see if it could be fixed. Seems like somebody might as well be enjoying it. I don't know if it's worth it, though. It's pretty mangy."

Between the crossed flaps of another box he could see a thin rectangle of turquoise lace. He pulled open the box and carefully lifted out a slender flamenco doll. "Okay then, remember this? She's good as new."

"Sure. I had her on my dresser until just a couple of years ago, remember?"

He looked around, feeling uncomfortably helpless. He started to open a box containing paper dolls but stopped. Whatever had happened, he wondered, to the paper dolls his sister had had from *Gone with the Wind?* Or the coloring books of Shirley Temple or Jane Withers or the Dionne Quintuplets? He wished that somewhere, in one of these boxes, he'd find the thick book of *Things to Do on a Rainy Day*. He wanted to see the pages and pages of puzzles and pictures, of things to color and cut out and paste. He wanted to remember how the cover looked and how the paper smelled. But he knew the book would never be there.

"Daddy," Libby was saying. "I don't really understand what you're doing."

He looked at her. He felt sick. "I guess I don't either," he said.

"I mean, what do you want me to do with all of this? Are we sorting it out or—"

A pile of boxes lodged in his mind. He wanted to open them but every time he imagined himself nearing them they seemed to jump to another place. "I don't know," he started saying. He felt Libby reach over and touch his hand.

"Daddy. What is it? I'll do anything you want."

He looked at her and wanted to hug her. The sick feeling that had swept over him was leaving, yet he felt weak. He put the flamenco doll back in the box with the tissue paper and the other dolls.

"You know," he said, sinking back against the couch and hearing his own voice as though it were coming from another room, "I guess I wanted to hang onto all of my things forever. You remember —I've told you about different things—the little wooden fort with all the lead Indians, the jigsaw puzzles I had, the game called Mr. Ree— things like that. Anyway, I kept them—most of them—stored in boxes down in the cellar of our old home in Bountiful." He thought of the big frame house with the wooden stairs that went down off the back porch and disappeared into darkness until you reached up and clicked on the little light bulb that hung overhead and then were suddenly surrounded by shelves of deep red jellies and purple jams, old bridles and dusty saddles. Piled against one wall were orange crates and bushel baskets, filled with broken lawn sprinklers, stray roller skates, and defunct Flit spray guns. And next to the old round washer, a torn bit of dusty black garden hose looped around its wringer, had been the boxes—some of them full of moldy textbooks from his older brothers and sisters, but most of them stuffed with the pieces and scraps of his own childhood.

"Why didn't you ever show them to me, Dad? Were they left in the house?"

"No," he shook his head. "No, they weren't left in the house." He remembered coming home from Montana, proud to be sixteen, tanned by the sun and feeling in his shoulders and chest and arms the effects of that summer on Uncle Royden's ranch. *We've decided to move to a smaller place now most of the kids are gone,* his father had written, and his arrival home had been just in time to help move the last few loads of furniture and belongings to the white house on Rosewood Avenue. The cellar had already been emptied by then, and even when his father told him that his brother-in-law had helped haul a lot of things to the dump, he had scarcely winced, trying too hard to be a man that summer to care about clinging to childish things.

"Your Uncle Cal—he helped Grandpa and Grandma move to the new house one summer while I was away working on a farm. He never did like the way Grandpa kept the cellar, and I think he just threw everything into the back of a truck and hauled it off to the dumpground."

He heard Libby make a little sound. Then: "How awful," she said. "*Someone* could have used them."

If he had not winced much that first afternoon in August when he discovered the cellar was bare, he had winced, more than once, the following week, and had finally taken the car and driven out to the city dump, searching for a trace of anything familiar. And as the years passed, he had spent hours pushing back through time trying to reconstruct in his mind the contents of the boxes. Even after he and Veda had married, he would think about the puppet or the Indians or the pictures of *Little Black Sambo* and feel as if he wanted to smash something. *What right does anyone have to throw part of another person's life away?* he had shouted at Veda once long ago, and he had made her keep everything of Libby's—the very first stuffed animals, the little cloth picture books, all the games and puzzles and dolls, everything.

Reaching out, he opened a small box that he knew contained her first books, and he picked one out, its pages limp and curled. "This was your first Mother Goose book—remember?"

"Daddy," she said quietly. "I guess it sounds awful, but I just don't think it means the same to me as it did to you." She glanced down, fumbling with the edge of her blouse, and then looked up, adding quickly, "I mean, maybe it's because I grew up with these things—and because even when I outgrew them, they were still there. I always knew where they were and Mom used to get them down for me once in a while. *You* even got them out sometimes—remember? I know they're mine and I like them okay, but I guess it's just different from how you seem to feel about all those things of yours—like the little Indians and stuff you used to talk about. Maybe just the idea of—"

"You know," he said, breaking in quietly, then pausing to take a breath and letting it out slowly, "maybe you're right. I guess maybe even if I found them now—stuffed off in some corner somewhere—they might not even be the way I remember them at all."

"Well, maybe—but that really wasn't what I meant. Maybe they'd seem more special than ever. Sometimes, Daddy, I've thought about you finding that book of yours—that rainy day book, you know, that you used to always tell me about—and I've thought how exciting it would be for you to have it again and be able to turn through the pages and remember all the hours you used to spend—"

He had thought of that too, and thinking of it now made something stir inside him.

"I wish it could be that way with some of *my* things, Daddy," she went on. "But it's just not the same. And I'm not really blaming you or Mom or—"

His eyes had drifted to the assortment of boxes surrounding them on the carpet. They *had* meant well, but somehow, she seemed to be right. He thought of the puppet, Clippo, and of the *Gulliver's Travels* songs that he had listened to, stretched out on the rug in front of the wind-up phonograph. And even while he helped her put the toys back in their boxes, even after she hugged him and told him, "I *do* love you, Daddy," he still thought a little about the fort and the Indians.

When she finally left to take the records back to Julie, calling from the car that she would see him at the hospital, he stood on the front porch a moment, then got in his own car and drove slowly back by the park. It was quieter there now, and he felt surprisingly at ease walking among the trees. He looked up at the leaves, the late afternoon light making them all the more golden, and he thought of Veda. And he thought too, for the first time, that now, maybe, he was ready to let her go.

Fugues and Improvisations: Variations on a Theme

When he tried later to recall whether it had been the name on the roll that first startled him or the sudden sight of her there, huddled self-conscious and out of place on the front row, he couldn't quite remember. He could not, however, forget—nor would he, in fact, ever be able to forget—the impact of suddenly pairing the name with the face—or the face with the name— knowing, with a slight shiver, that the days ahead were going to be noticeably different.

It was early September, and the students, skin browned and hair bleached by the sun, had trickled into the classroom still trailing shreds of summer. But the pallid and angular form caught like a wintry branch in the center seat before him had seemed apart, remote. Her moles and wrinkles had been dusted with a fine layer of powder; and, resisting time or season, her gray hair had been pushed neatly into tight familiar furrows. In the midst of white-surf smiles and hair that swished like honey-colored grass, she had seemed a relic, cast up on the shore by an indifferent sea.

He remembered how he had looked down at the sheet of paper that had been passed around the room while he arranged the stereophonic equipment for his usual introductory lecture in Music 101, and how that one name, written in round and wobbly letters, had almost leaped up, from among the blur of Kathys and Steves and Vickies, to unnerve him: Sariah Euphelda Mangum Pedersen. He was accustomed to unusual names and often took them home to share with Joan while they sat at the table eating and coaxing the children to finish their last bites. There had been a Thai student one semester named Jit Nagapradip, a Navajo girl named Ramona Red Elk, even a sad little soul from Florida named Livia Goope. But this particular name—partly, he decided, because of its appropriateness for that remnant of another century that had, quite unexpectedly, turned up on the front row—had seemed somehow foreboding, even threatening, from that first moment, the way the other names, however curious, never had.

He was not sure why. He had, as a matter of fact, been wondering why, sitting in his office with the class roll spread out on the desk before him, when a soft knocking startled him and he glanced up to find himself staring at the tall bony figure in the long coat who stood, looking lost and apologetic, in the partly opened doorway.

"Excuse me, Dr. Christenson," he heard her say in a voice barely audible, and he motioned for her to come inside and sit down. "I don't want but a minute of your time," she went on, sitting on the edge of the chair and fumbling with the big purse propped on her knees, "but I'm Sadie Pedersen and—uh—" Her eyes shifted down to her purse as she bit at her lip, then she went on: "You know, Dr. Christenson, it's just a dream-come-true for me to get to come to school at all at my age—"

"How old are you?" he found himself asking before he could help himself.

She blinked; then she took a deep breath and exhaled, "I'm sixty-seven," looking at him as though she were awaiting some reaction. He was unaware of what registered on his face or what exactly she had expected to see there, but no age between sixty and eighty would have surprised him: she was, after all, unquestionably *old.* "Yessir," she went on quietly, giving an almost palsied series of little nods. "Sixty-seven—and sixty-eight on March eighteenth."

He glanced at the rollbook to avoid her gaze, and decided to shift the subject. "Did I understand you to say *Sadie* Pedersen?"

She had evidently noticed his eyes on the roll, for she suddenly bent forward, adjusted the rimless glasses on her nose, and then pushed one trembling bony finger over the longest name on the list. "Sariah Euphelda Pedersen," she said. "Sariah Euphelda *Mangum* Pedersen."

He shifted in his swivel chair, feeling oddly as though a little boy still squirmed inside his associate-professor shell. "I—uh—generally call the students by their first names," he finally managed, "but—uh—if you'd prefer—"

Something passed over her face, and he sensed behind her thin closed lips a perceptible grinding of back teeth as she weighed out what he was asking. Her knobby fingers fidgeted with her purse while her neck, the skin taut against the cords, twisted and stretched an extra inch or two above the collar of her coat.

"Oh," she said, biting first one lip and then the other and looking down at the clasp of her purse that didn't seem to catch, "I think Sister Pedersen would be—fine—" She glanced up then, adding quickly, "—if you wouldn't mind."

He felt embarrassed, and, unable to envision himself calling her anything *but* Sister Pedersen, wondered why he had even brought it up. Perhaps it was a carry-over from his attempt at home, along with Joan, to put into practice Dr. Ginott's theory of giving children choices—only now *he* felt like the child.

He found himself searching for something to say. "Of course—that would be fine." He glanced back at the roll and must have moved his lips as he read the names once again to himself, for he heard her pronounce them aloud: "Sariah Euphelda Mangum Pedersen."

Euphelda, she told him, had been her mother's name; Mangum, her maiden name; and the Sariah, for as long as she could remember, had always been shortened simply to Sadie. She had been, she went on to say in her tired quiet voice, the second oldest girl of fourteen children and had grown up on a little ranch in southeastern Idaho. When she was eleven, the family had lost their farm and moved to Koosharem, Utah. A year later her mother had died of diphtheria, leaving the care of the younger children to her and her sister who, within a year or two, fell ill with typhoid fever and was buried alongside the mother in the spring. She had stayed by her father and helped to raise the little ones until the youngest was nine, and then, one wintry day in 1921, she left Koosharem to marry Nels Pedersen, a widower with four children, and began the life that, for the next forty-nine years, would bind her to the little farm a few miles north of Alpine.

He felt uncomfortable knowing so much of her background, as if this knowledge were beginning to augur some vague obligation that he might be unwilling to fulfill. Yet he was curious, at the same time, to know more—to know why she was here at BYU and what she intended to gain by taking his class. He tried to formulate a question, but she interrupted his thoughts, as though she had read his mind.

"I'm majoring, Dr. Christenson," she said slowly and carefully, "in genealogy."

"Oh," was all he could say, but he managed an agreeable nodding of his head.

It was her great love, she told him. She liked keeping records; she liked searching through the files for names of her ancestors. And she loved studying the scriptures. She loved studying of any kind— if only her eyes would hold out. "I used to read a book a week," she told him, but then went on to tell how helping the boys with their arithmetic and helping the girls get their reports had eaten away all her time. "But I don't begrudge it," she said. "No siree, not a minute of it. They've all been good students—pret'near straight A, every one of 'em, except our youngest boy, and—well —he's a good boy too. He's not so good with his lessons and things like that, but he can tell you anything you want to know about cars. Oh my, he can take a car apart and put it back together like nobody's business. He's a regular humdinger, when it comes to motors and things like that, I'll tell you." She breathed a long sigh and stared at her purse, running her bony fingers along its worn edges. Then she looked at him steadily and announced slowly, putting great emphasis on every word: "I've raised eleven children, not counting my brothers and sisters I took care of when I was a girl. Yessir, eleven of 'em and every one of 'em's got him a good education and a good job—except the two we've still got to home that helps us with the chores and all."

There were eight boys and three girls, she told him—three boys and a girl belonging to Nels and his first wife, all of them married and settled around the country; one boy of her brother's they had raised after his folks had been killed one winter when their pickup overturned coming into town from the farm; two girls and two boys of their own, scattered with their families from Fort Leonard Wood, Missouri, to Manila, Utah; and their last two boys, Derrold, 27, and Bert J., 19, who were still at home.

She went on to tell him how difficult it had been, the last few years, keeping up the farm, how the early frosts the year before had taken the whole potato crop, and how the heavy rains the following spring had damaged the wheat. She must have sensed that his mind was beginning to wander for she suddenly straightened her back, took in a deep breath that she let out again with some finality, and then stood up, her fingers still working busily at her purse.

"Well," she said, "I don't mean to take all your time, Dr. Christenson. I just wanted to let you know I'm just thrilled to pieces to be able to come. I've wanted to do it for a long time, and Nels told me I could if I would just keep my health up and not let it get me down. It'll be a little bit of a struggle," she warned him, "because I've been away from the schoolroom for almost fifty years. It wasn't until after I was married a while that I finally finished up my high school courses—I had to drop out, you see, and help out at home—but I finally got me my diploma and, Dr. Christenson, I'll tell you that's just meant the world to me. I know it doesn't sound like much, but it was a struggle, with the kids and all, and I'm just as proud of that as I could be of anything." She sighed again and then looked at him directly. "I just want you to understand that I might have a hard time keeping up with these youngsters, but Nels says I've got a lot of gumption, and I'll sure try to keep up with all the work. I'll be taking a full load, but I need to get me some other credits, they said, and I thought this music appreciation course sounded so interesting, and I'm sure it will be. I just love music, Dr. Christenson; I even used to be able to pick out chords on the piano before my hands got so knotted up like this, but anyway"—and again she gave the succession of little nervous nods—"I'll be doing my best to do all the reading and get up there to the library and listen to those different pieces. It's Beethoven, isn't it, for Wednesday?"

"Mozart," he corrected. "Mozart's *Symphony Number Forty*."

"Oh yes, Mozart." She pronounced it Moze-art. She started to fumble with some papers in her purse. "Well, I suppose I've got it written down here somewhere. Anyway, thank you, Dr. Christenson, for your time, and if you'll just bear with me, I'll sure be doing my best." She held out a hand, and he leaped up to accept it; then she was gone.

October was chillier than usual. An early snow surprised the leaves, hastening their transition from buttery yellow to a dull, dry rust. Almost overnight, the mountains turned dun-colored, and where the rugged outline of Timpanogos had cut a clean crisp line across the blue sky only a week before, a watercolor gray now seeped down behind the foothills, fuzzing contours and gradually obscuring all. There were days when, overhead, the entire sky seemed to billow like a bleached sheet on some unseen clothesline, and the trees would shiver and rustle like a rattlesnake, the black branches suddenly convulsing, jerking in wild spasms, their dark damp leaves slapping against each other and finally slipping away to fall brown and wet along the sidewalk and on the cars parked beside the gutter.

Although he could not always put his finger on the exact reason for it, the old joy of teaching Music 101 seemed to be uncomfortably lacking this semester. He could still recall, with little difficulty, the excitement he had felt seven years before when, fresh from graduate school, he had introduced his first 101 class to the glories of classical music. It had not been an especially easy one, that first semester; yet, with the possible exception of a few students—the electrical engineering student, for example, who claimed he played too much Purcell and Haydn and Mozart, and the tall girl with stringy hair who never learned to like Purcell or Gluck—he felt comparatively successful. "You can't win them all," a colleague had told him, and he had come, finally, to believe it was true. The last few years, however, had, in some ways, been even more difficult than the first; and now, with the present semester already six weeks underway, he feared that he was facing the greatest challenge yet.

There are classes and *classes*, he had tried to console himself. Sometimes his little witticisms broke the ice the first day; other semesters he still felt halfway through the term as though he would never get to know the students usurping the desks occupied another semester by faces warmer and more docile. Yet usually by the end, the faces, however impenetrable at first, had gradually dissolved into three-dimensional beings with individual tastes and peculiarities—people, in effect, that he cared about. He looked forward to this—yet, having had to fail three of those very live and very real individuals at the end of the past semester, the anticipation was not without some tinge of discomfort.

The problem this semester had something to do with the four

football players who sat together on the back row, biceps bulging from their shirtsleeves, their Levied legs sprawled in the aisles. Since the first class period, they had never all been present on the same day, but the ones attending invariably huddled together, mumbling comments back and forth out of the corners of their mouths, and groaning audibly whenever he mentioned anything heavier than *Peter and the Wolf* or *Flight of the Bumblebee*. It also had something to do with the mousy little blond girl on the front row whose inevitable hand waving in the air was forever visible out of the corner of his eye and who thought she had some sort of "in" with him because, she clearly informed him after one of the first class periods, she had had seven years of piano—to say nothing of four years of ballet and tap—and dearly loved *Clair de Lune* and *Moonlight Sonata*.

But most of all it had to do with Sadie M. Pedersen. She had been faithful in attending class, having missed only once or twice so far and then having taken great pains to call him long distance from Alpine with extended apologies and detailed explanations. But she had not done well on her quizzes; and though she paid the strictest attention in class, leaning forward in her desk with her head turned slightly as though her left ear were better than her right, her eyes narrowed and her head nodding as she ostensibly digested every word, he felt certain that the whole thing was inaccessibly beyond her grasp.

One cold morning, a thin frost whitening the yellowed grass, he pushed through the glass doors of the Harris Fine Arts Center, his arms loaded with books and corrected mid-term exams, and climbed the stairs to find her waiting on a bench outside his door. Her eyes looked watery and the end of her nose was a pinkish violet. A man's brown and maroon woolen scarf was muffled loosely around her neck and chin. With her hand trembling in its woolen glove, she pulled down a corner of the scarf and croaked something unintelligible.

"Are you all right?" he asked, bracing his books and papers against the wall as he sought with a free hand for the key in his pocket.

"No," she answered in a hoarse whisper. "I'm not all right." A

161

gloved hand fluttered to her forehead, and she shook her head slowly. "No. That's what I came about."

He found the key and pushed open the door, motioning for her to step inside. She sat down, a stack of books making a little pyramid in her lap.

"Nels didn't want me to come today," she said as he put his things down and took off his coat, "but my ride came for me and I thought I'd better come and get my examination paper." She glanced up at him and, as if reading something on his face, went on quickly: "Oh, I know it was awful. I shouldn't've come at all that day being as how I could feel this cold coming on even then." She stopped to cough several times into a wadded pink Kleenex. "Oh, I'm just ashamed at what I must've done. And I knew those pieces too."

He sank into his swivel chair and touched the group of tests, wondering where hers was. It had been bad; her score, he remembered, was something like 37 out of 100.

"Oh, I studied, Dr. Christenson. You wouldn't know it from that, but I spent hours and hours up in that listening room . . ." He knew it was probably true. Twice in the last week he had dropped into the Learning Resource Center to check out or return records, and she had been there both times, bundled up in her coat, her tired face seemingly distorted and elongated by the grotesque earphones pressing against her temples. "I just couldn't get my mind to working," she went on. "I heard them pieces, every one of them just as familiar as could be, but I couldn't for the life of me place which name went with which. I know I got that *Messiah* one. We've sung that at church." He had found her paper and glanced at the Listening Identification page. She had missed the Messiah one too; she had put Haydn instead of Handel. "But some of those others," she went on, "I tell you I was just so nervous and upset and my eraser wouldn't work and Lord knows what I finally went and put."

He hated to give her the paper with the big *E* grade marked on the front page. Perhaps *E* seemed a softer way of communicating failure than *F*, but there was finally no way to cushion the message. He glanced at the other pages. She had failed the Fill-in-the-Blank, the Matching, the Multiple Choice, the True and False. And she had failed without question the Listening Identification.

"I don't think I done quite so bad where we had to match the composer with the history part, and I didn't feel so bad about the true and false, but my head was so full of cold pills and dizziness that I couldn't get my mind going at all when it come to that other. I think I put the Beethoven on the Bach and the Bach on the Beethoven and Lord knows what all."

He slid the test across the desk so that it rested in front of her. She stared at it for a moment, as though she had never seen it before, lifted up one of the pages with a shaky hand, and then pushed it away from her a few inches. "Well," she said, and her chest seemed to collapse as she let out a long breath. "I just knew it wasn't good. I shouldn't've come at all that day."

It was too late to advise her to drop. It was impossible to think that she might do remarkably better in the remaining half of the semester, yet there *would* be more quizzes—and the final. He shifted uneasily in his seat as she coughed again into the Kleenex and then said hoarsely, "I don't even want to take this home."

He fingered the edges of the other tests. "I can understand that," he heard himself say.

"Do you know," she began slowly, emphasizing each word, and then paused as if awaiting his complete attention. He looked up at her to assure her she had it. "Do you know, Dr. Christenson, what it's like to have to take an examination paper like this home to your husband and your grown children?"

He may have blinked, but he refused to avert his gaze. What was she asking? He would not let her back him into a corner.

"My children was every one an *A* student—like I said, except for the youngest one. And the grandchildren, too—they're regular whizzes, all of 'em." She swallowed, looking down as her quivering fingers began picking the wad of Kleenex into little pink shreds. "What would they think of their grandma if they knew?" Then, as though her eyes finally realized what her fingers had been doing to the Kleenex, she brushed the little pieces of pink tissue from her lap and held them in a wad in her hand. "Dr. Christenson," she said, "I don't want to be putting you to extra trouble, but I was wondering if it would be asking too much to let me take this over? When I feel better, I mean. I shouldn't've no more come that day than I should've got out of bed to come here today, but I wanted to talk to you and see what you thought because I had a good hunch I done awful—although I was hoping it wasn't quite so awful as this—and I know if I could just get my health up and clear my head out a mite, I could do a darn sight better."

He found himself rubbing one side of his face and finding a spot the razor had missed. His eyes fell on her exam: 37 out of 100. She had, he realized, got 37 right. She had missed 63, true, and missing more than half of the questions seemed to warrant a failing grade; yet the fact that she had actually answered 37 correctly suddenly swept over him like a revelation. Thirty-seven different questions answered correctly. Surely that was *some* kind of an accomplishment and should be worth *something*.

"All right," he said suddenly, surprising himself. "As soon as you feel up to it, come in and talk to me and we'll see what we can do."

Her eyes grew more bleary and she started to cough into her hand, but when she finished she tried to smile. "I just know I can do better if I can just get on top of this cold. Nels says I've got to watch my health first of all, and I guess I've just got to mind him." She dabbed at her eyes with the pink wad in her hand. "Thank you for your time, Dr. Christenson. And I'll sure be doing my darnedest." It took her a few minutes to gather up her books and her purse, and then she was gone.

The days passed by quickly, like the leaves of an old calendar shuffled by a cold wind. There were bleak mornings when he entered into the classroom's warm stuffiness and found the chair-desk waiting empty on the front row. But the explanations followed without fail: "My arthritis was acting up and Nels put me right to bed," her frail voice apologized long distance from Alpine, "but I'll try to get me a ride up there over the weekend and do my listening"; "She's got a bad tooth, and we've got to get her in to the dentist," Nels himself called once to say, asking if he could take her assignment over the phone; "We've had us some family problems," read the quivering letters of a note written in pencil and slid under his door. But most of the time she was there, bundled up in the big coat and scarf. And he saw her in the library's listening room, her eyes seeming to drift unseeingly as she concentrated on the sounds coming through the earphones; and once he noticed her sitting alone in the back of the Madsen Recital Hall, stifling a cough into a handkerchief while a graduate student performed on a cello on the stage below.

One gray morning, with the Thanksgiving holidays only a week away, he stopped her after class, her eyes weary and a shopping bag full of books clutched in her arms. Had she forgotten about the test, he wanted to know. No, she had not forgotten, but there had been problems: one son, the one in Denver, was in the hospital with hepatitis; a grandson from Smithfield was going to have to go back to the hospital in Salt Lake for another operation on his hip; and their youngest boy, Bert J., had found him a girlfriend in Lindon and thought he wanted to get married right away, and they didn't know what they were going to do if he left home right now with things in such a muddle the way they were and her only a junior in high school on top of that. Well, he was sorry to hear about all of their bad luck, but he wanted to make certain that, if she were really going to take the test over, she wouldn't put it off for so long that she would end up compromising her final. Yes, he was right, she knew that, but things were already piling up on her in her religion classes until she could hardly see her way out, but maybe she could put her shoulder to the wheel and get her a ride into Provo over the weekend and listen to those tapes a few more times and then maybe on Monday—

On Monday morning she was there beside his office door while the sky outside was still a frosty indigo. He had forgotten the appointment and would not have been there at that hour at all if he had not set his alarm early in order to arrive a few hours before class to do some work on a paper he was writing concerning a comparison of liturgical and secular polyphonic music of the German school in the late 16th century.

"Well," she said, shaking her head slowly, "I don't know as I'm any more ready than I was before, but I listened till I got such a pain in my head I couldn't hardly get to sleep at all."

"Did you review all your notes and the old test?" he asked. And he remembered then that he had intended to prepare a slightly altered version of the original test, but had forgotten. Unfortunately, he would have to give her the same one over.

"Oh, I know the answers. If I can just get my head working now. There was a time, Dr. Christenson, I could recite 'Hiawatha' and 'Evangeline' and—oh, I can't remember all the others, but my memory now"—and she shook her head, sighing deeply—"it's just not what it was. Nothing like what it was."

He gave her the exam, resenting the time it took to relocate the tapes and spot the various passages in the pieces they were required to know. He watched her shaky hand as she wrote. Frequently she ran a hand through the gray wisps of hair that strayed within her eyesight while she marked down her answers. Sometimes she tapped out the rhythm in the air with her pencil.

When she finished, he quickly went over the test while she waited, growing more and more uneasy at the number of red marks he was forced to put on each page. "I can't for the life of me keep it all in my head," she was saying, shaking her head. "I can remember clear as a bell standing up in front of my class and reciting 'Snow-Bound' when I was just a little bitty thing. And I love music. We always had music up home when I was a little girl. Mama played the organ, and Dad the violin. He could even get a tune out of an ordinary saw—jew's harp, anything. And, oh my, how he could play the banjo!"

She sighed. "No, it's not that I don't love music." She held up a bony hand. "These hands, Dr. Christenson—would you believe I used to play the piano? I never had time—nor the money—for proper lessons, but I could pick me out a tune, and I used to chord for the children." She took a long breath, raising her eyebrows, closing her eyes; then she opened them and sighed. "Yessir, it's not that I don't love music. When the kids was little, we had us a Victrola and we used to have all the music of Victor Herbert. I can remember we had *The Red Mill* too, and Jeanette McDonald singing 'Alice Blue Gown'—and I think we had *The William Tell Overture* and all of them. I suspect we've still got some of them in the basement somewhere, although most of them got broke, and the Victrola went on the blink a long time ago and Nels finally had to haul it out to the dump." She stared at the exam and then looked up at him. "Derrold told me the other day he was going to get me tickets to see *The Nutcracker* ballet here at the University this winter, and I was just thrilled to death. They all know how I'm taking this course and how we have to go to so many recitals and things to get credit so they want to help me all they can."

He had completed marking the last page, and as he flipped back through the test, counting up the red marks, he was aware of her eyes on him and imagined he heard her mumbling, whispering to herself. The final score was 46—only slightly better than the one previous. From the corner of his eye he could see her shaking her head, one hand nervously fingering her cheek, her chin, her lips. She had still missed more than half; the test, then, was still a failure. But how did one acknowledge to her the increase of nine points? He hesitated, sensing that her eyes were trying to look and yet not look at his hand holding the red pencil falteringly over her test. Then, quickly, he marked *D–* at the top of the page.

She seemed to flinch a little. "Do you know," she said, "I think I could tell you the name of every one of those composers if you just wouldn't ask me? Now I probably went and marked the whole thing completely the opposite, but listen to me—Beethoven now, isn't he the one that has those violins making such a fuss? And the other one—oh, what's his name—I can just hear it. Listen—I can sing you the whole thing. Haydn, isn't it?" And with a series of little "dum-te-dums," she began tapping her toe and singing, not the second-movement theme from Haydn's *Surprise Symphony* as he had expected, but a melody he recognized as Dvorak's "Humoresque," which had not even been on the test.

"You see?" she said, her eyes pleading. "I could sing every one of them for you. It's just that my mind goes completely haywire when it comes to using a pencil and getting it down on those examinations." She had picked up her exam and was nervously rolling it up as she talked.

He felt drained. It was nearly time for class and he had to gather his notes and locate whatever records or tapes he might need. What could he tell her? With final exams less than three weeks away, any noticeable change in her grade seemed doubtful—seemed, in effect, impossible. He hoped that the teachers in her other courses could be more encouraging.

"How are you doing in the rest of your classes?" he found himself asking.

"Well," she said, tipping her head sideways and smacking her lips before going on, "I'll tell you, Dr. Christenson, it's a struggle. I'm doing my darnedest to keep up, and I hope to get maybe a B or a C in my Introduction to Genealogy. Now I haven't done so well in my history course, but if I can get my work caught up, maybe I won't be so bad off in my theology class. I'm sixty-seven, you know, and I'm having a devil of a time keeping up with these youngsters. But if I can just keep my health up, I think I'll make it. I just need to get enough credits to get my certificate, and your class just sounded so interesting and I've always loved music so and—"

"Well," he cut in, gathering up a manila folder and ushering her toward the door, "do your best, and we'll see what happens." But he felt empty, weak, for he felt that he knew what would happen.

The days grew colder. On his desk the papers mingled chaotically, burying the little calendar with its unturned pages neglected, forgotten. He had looked forward, almost impatiently, to each Saturday in November; now, in December, the day loomed at the end of each week as bleakly as Monday cast its gray shadow over the beginning. Saturday now signalled morning hours bent over the typewriter composing exams, and afternoons caught in the tangle of snow-topped cars circling parking lots and creeping, bumper-to-bumper, down tinsel-garlanded Center Street in search of an empty space.

On one such Saturday in mid-December, after noting Mrs. Pedersen's absence for almost a week, he thought he saw her on the street. Waiting inside his car at a red light while the windshield wipers slapped at the wet falling snow and, beside him, Joan leaned over the back seat to separate the boys' argument over who deserved the most for Christmas, he noticed ahead of them the familiar brown coat and the spindly legs struggling to get out of a faded car. A tall old man with a disarray of gray hair and a ruddy, bony face was reaching in to take her by the arm. So that's Nels, he thought, peering through the blurred windshield at the bent figure who was obviously even older than his wife. From around the side of the car came a boy in a plaid Mackinaw, blowing on his hands and rubbing them together, and the two of them, the boy and the old man, each took an arm and guided her across the icy street. They disappeared into a brick complex where doctors and dentists kept their offices. He had meant to tell Joan, "There she is—the Sadie Pedersen I've told you about from my class," but something about the little scene momentarily stunned him, and before he could get the words out, the three of them had disappeared. But the scene lingered with him: while they pushed through the crowds in J. C. Penney's and Sears and Taylor's—even waiting in the line, hours later, at Grand Central's checkout counter—he was bothered by the image and uneasy that his own life seemed somehow entangled with hers.

When, on Monday morning, he looked up from his desk and saw the face, he could not, for a moment, place it. He had heard the knock, called out his perfunctory "Come in," and then gone about searching for the paper he was missing. But when he looked up and saw the old man in the doorway, his face strangely familiar and yet unfamiliar, he must have stared several seconds before he remembered where he had seen him. In that instant of recognition, however, he felt an icy wave ripple down his back and his stomach's attempt to dodge it.

"I'm Nels Pedersen," he heard the old fellow say at the same time that his mind made the same announcement.

"Have a seat," he heard his own voice say weakly, his heart pounding in his ears and in the back of his head. *Something has happened to her,* he thought, the old lady's tired face flashing before him. *He's come to tell me that she's—*

"Sadie asked me to bring by some of her reports that's due and get whatever reading assignment she's behint on. She's laid up there to home and not feeling worth a darn."

A warm current of relief went through him. "What is it? Anything serious?"

"Well, she's got arthritis and diabetes and every other thing you can name, but she's mainly just give out—and she's got her a good cold too. I give her the dickens for traipsin' off over here every day of the week, rain or shine, Saturdays included, but she's got her mind set on gettin' her that degree, and come hell or high water, it looks like she's bound and determined to do it. She got it in her head she was going to get up and come over here today, but I made her stay put in bed. She's worried sick about how she's gonna do in your class but she says to tell you she'll be here Wednesday without fail."

"There is no class Wednesday. Tomorrow's the last day of classes, and then we start finals. Her final, Music 101, will be . . ."—and he ran his finger down the exam schedule spread open on his desk— ". . . Saturday. This coming Saturday at ten A.M." He hesitated. "She'll need to have finished the text and be able to identify everything on these three handouts plus those she's already got." He reached out the three dittoed sheets and watched the old farmer's face, expecting some reaction, although he was not sure what. Did her husband—did she herself, *did anyone*—think she could possibly pass? Had she told him what her grades had been? Had she—

"She's sure hopin' to get her a C in here," he heard the old man say. "In fact, she's got to have her a C from what I can get out of it, in order to get her whatchamacallit. I know she's had quite a little bit of trouble gettin' caught up with the work 'n' all, but she's sure had her hands full, I can tell you that." The old fellow looked down at the papers he held in his hands; then he looked up. "Well, anyway, I hope she can get her C, like she needs. We sure do appreciate the time you've took with her and—well—I guess that about takes care of it then." He stood up and stretched out a large freckled hand with white hair on the knuckles. "Sure do want to thank you. And I hope you can help her out." He had trouble turning around and finding the door, but finally he was gone, and Christenson was left feeling a great hollowness inside. It was odd; the wave of relief that had swept over him only moments before had now ebbed away, and a new wave, cold and threatening, seemed about to crash down upon his numbness.

More than once in his life he had awakened exhausted from a dream in which he suddenly found himself on a stage, realizing, as the curtain went up, that he did not know his part, and he was forced to linger near the curtains to repeat the whispered words of the prompter, or make frequent exits into the wings to search for the script in panic, trying frantically to commit to memory whatever lines or fragments of lines might get him through the next few minutes of terror. He had associated the dream, at one time, with his years at graduate school, when being a music major had grown into something more than simply striving to be a competent oboist in the orchestra, and he had felt suddenly inundated by the plethora of dates and facts and theories required of him as a doctor of music. But shortly after he had started teaching, all that had subsided. He had, however, begun to feel smothered by something else. He had adjusted to his role as teacher, had come, in fact, to feel comfortable in that realm of music that involved less time in the practice room and more in the library; but he had not felt prepared for the role of great arbiter that seemed, more and more, each semester, to thrust itself, unbidden, upon him. Why the dream came back to him now he was not sure; the details were not the same, the situation no longer applicable. But it was the desperation, the panic. It was not so much a feeling of being unprepared for the role as it was an anxiety born out of having to play a role he had never expected.

He thought of the three students he had failed last spring. It was not his fault they had not passed; he refused to take the blame for that. Furthermore, he refused to let it upset his year. If Kristen had become negligent—concerned more with the appearance of her long, almost platinum, hair or with the demands of the pimpled boy that leaned, entangled with her, against the wall by the drinking fountain than she was with the class itself—was it his fault? If she started out with a B, then got a D, and finally disappeared entirely the last two weeks of class, was he to blame? If Melvin left school for almost three weeks—for what he later called "personal problems at home"—and then reappeared repentant and gushing with promises but proved finally incapable of making up the work satisfactorily, was he to answer? And Ramona Red Elk. Why should he feel responsible if Ramona hovered on the brink of a $D-$ in every test, every quiz, yet kept coming—unlike Ervin Ironleggings or whatever his name had been, who had been wise enough to drop—to finally make the lowest score of the whole class on the final exam? Would it have been right to pass her? Perhaps the final score would have come out to be another $D-$, but would that have been enough? Should he have given her the $D-$ and let her pass? He refused to dwell on that. He would not.

But now there was Sadie Pedersen. Just a few minutes before, the possibility of—of some misfortune had left him weak, drained, empty. There had been something leaden, something cold and heavy, in that sudden possibility of finality, some unbearable weight in that momentary sensation of helplessness, in the chilling realization of one's ability to revoke or alter or make amends. Then, in a matter of seconds, the old man's words had erased all that. But now what? For now the problem was larger than ever. The light, no longer red, was flashing green: but what was it that could be revoked, altered, amended?

The week whirled to an end in a blizzard of icy flakes and swirling papers, damp and reeking of ditto fluid. Saturday—and the Music 101 final—came; and as the old man had promised, she was there, still in her coat, coughing into her handkerchief and running her quivering fingers over the side of her face as she wrote, then erased, wrote, and erased again. She was the last one to finish, the last to leave, and she paused by his desk, after she had gathered up her books and her purse, leaning her sunken eyes and cheeks down close to his and speaking in a whisper wasted in the empty room.

It took him a moment to fully realize that he had actually heard what she said: "Well, it looks like I'm going to be having me a wedding. Bert J. and Orva Sue's set on getting themselves married before Christmas, and there doesn't seem to be any talking them out of it. So," she said, breathing out and straightening her back, "with her mother abed with multiple sclerosis, I'm up to here helping the poor thing get some kind of trousseau together." She shook her head, then gave his arm a little pat. "Well, I don't know how I done on this one, Dr. Christenson, but I tell you I listened to every one of those tapes till I was blue in the face. And studied the book backwards and forwards on top of that."

He shifted uneasily. Her quivering hand still rested on his coat sleeve. "Well," she said, "if I can just get me a C, I'll pull through," and she raised two crooked fingers, crossed as though they had grown that way, and shook them at him slightly. "And I sure do thank you for your patience with me. Music was always one of my greatest loves."

He said something to her, he was sure of that later, but even as she went out and he sat numb and shivering, listening to her coughing down the hall, he could not remember what it was.

His office light was one of the few lights in the Harris Fine Arts Center still burning after midnight on Thursday, the day before final grades were due. He had sat for a long time without moving, staring at the machine-scored answer sheet before him, the name Sariah M. Pedersen written shakily above the columns of blue numbers where her answers had been blacked in with pencil. She had failed the final, that was certain. With a score of 77 out of a possible 160, there was no way he could even rightfully give her a D. "She doesn't have the faintest idea what a melisma is," he told himself aloud, "or who Orlando di Lasso was." And her answers, as far as he could tell, indicated a real confusion between Beethoven and Bach, Haydn and Handel. The directions clearly warned against any extraneous writing on the answer sheet, yet he thought he could make out, though mostly erased, a note she had scribbled to herself in the margin beside answer 97 in the identification section: "Lovely and soothing." That would be Tchaikovsky. At least she got that one right.

He looked down at the prepared sheets and carbons on which he had to write in a final grade beside each IBM-printed name. Only one was still left blank: PEDERSEN, SARIAH EUPHE. He could see her, in his imagination, painstakingly tatting the edge of a pillowslip—or intently crocheting doilies to go on the arms of bulky chairs—for Bert J. and his new wife. But he could also see her hovering over his desk with her tired face; hear her cough echoing down the hall; imagine, even, he saw her lying against white sheets and breathing raspily.

Why did they invade him with their lives? He got up and walked around the room. He had to fail her. He had no choice. Arguments rose up in his mind; a defense seemed necessary. He felt suddenly as though the walls of his office were growing thin, disappearing, and in their place a surrounding sea of faces peered down on him. *I need at least a D or I can't stay in school:* Ramona Red Elk's voice, echoing back through the days. *But I had to leave school for a while*—Melvin now, wide-eyed, pleading—*because of what happened back home*—

What *had* happened at home? Crop failure? An unexpected operation? His father had deserted the mother and children? Jailed for embezzlement? Suicide? He wished he had pressed the boy to find out—yet he was not entirely certain he wanted to know, for the knowing shouldn't change anything, should it? What did it all matter? What did any of it, finally, have to do with him and with Music 101? Haydn and Mozart and Bach and J. Stewart Christenson were something quite apart from all that, weren't they?

He turned nervously, searching the blur of books on the shelves for the faces that had been there, staring down at him. He had thought he heard a question—*If you can give her a C, then couldn't you have*—but before he could prepare an argument, the questioner was gone. It was as though the lights had come up on some vast auditorium and found the seats empty. He felt a sudden wave of loneliness sweep over him. Where was Ramona Red Elk this fall? Melvin? Kristen? What had happened to them? What were they doing?

He turned back to the desk and stared at the empty space beside the name glaring back at him. There should be no wavering now, no weakening. He would do what he had to do, what he had done to Ramona, to Melvin, to Kristen, what he had had to do previously to the others whose names—unlike their haunting faces—no longer came to him. There had to be *some* gauge, *some* limit, *some* justice. He sat down, hesitated a moment, then ran his pencil along the name in his rollbook to the last column and carefully marked *E* in the empty space.

But the name stared back at him. He could feel eyes on him. And yet, somehow, he felt desperately alone, as though a ship had just pulled away in the night, leaving him abandoned on some distant rocky shore. Somewhere in the building someone coughed, and he felt himself flinch. A face rose up before him, and he flinched again under the tired gaze, the sunken eyes, the crooked fingers that flitted over the wrinkled cheek. He got up from the desk, a rush of dizziness coming over him. It was late. He had to go home. Yet the pencil, he realized, was still in his hand; he had not yet entered the grade on the final roll. *I am sixty-seven years old,* a voice reminded him quietly, and he felt his knees weaken. He turned back to look at the long pale green sheet with the one empty space, his pencil tapping a rapid tattoo against the metallic edge of the desk. A feeling of anger awakened and squirmed inside him, and he let the pencil fly from his fingers and strike the tidiness of the waiting grade sheet. He turned and paced the room, his hands thrust now in his pockets, fumbling with the keys and bits of loose change. Suddenly he whirled, faced the desk, stared once more at the name that would not let go, then impulsively took up the pencil and heavily filled in the space under the letter C. He looked at it, his pencil still hesitating above the mark, then he quickly erased it and brusquely blacked in the square next to it: C−.

He felt lighter, relieved, as he put on his overcoat; he even felt somehow clean, his heart beating rapidly, as he went down the stairs, pushed open the glass doors, and stepped out into the chilly night air. The quad was deserted. A new skirt of snow covered all. Yet, as he moved around the side of the building to the empty parking lot where his car looked stranded like some frozen straggler in an arctic expanse, a faint sound, a rhythmic clinking-squeaking, broke the stillness and caused him to look back. A big hulk of a boy, awkwardly hunched over the handlebars and wearing a wool cap and earmuffs, laboriously pedaled by, clutching his books precariously against his coat and huffing great puffs of steam like someone gasping for air in a cold black sea. Christenson felt an inexplicable surge of sadness sweep over him, though he did not know the boy.

He hurried to his car, quickly fitted his key into the icy lock and ducked inside. The wipers were stuck midway on the frosted windshield, and the engine would not start. He wiggled the key nervously in the ignition and pumped with futility at the pedal beneath his foot. It was no use. He stepped out and locked the door, then turned in the night toward home. He walked briskly at first, then started running, his steps making hollow sounds on the icy pavement. His breath came in sharp gasps now, and though he didn't look back to see, he shivered with the odd sensation that there were other footsteps echoing behind him.

Light Switch

I never meant to electrocute my sister, but that didn't stop me from feeling awful about it for days after. In fact, I *still* feel terrible about it, if I let my mind start thinking about those things. And sometimes a smell alone will do it. Like autumn leaves. You might not think they have much of a smell at all, but they really do. There's a September smell that's noticeable by the first or second week and then gets heavier along towards the end of the month. It's still a dry smell, no question about it, but it's richer and moister than the end-of-October smell, which, of course, is still a long way from how November smells when the leaves are almost dust and the air just hangs there, cold and waiting.

And now I'm thinking about that again, which is really a lot worse than remembering the dream about my sister because it really happened. Although I guess that's debatable. Whether it's worse, I mean, because there's not much question about whether it happened or not. The man's dead and I was the one who found him; it's that simple. But I guess that's not true either, because it isn't quite as simple as I'd sometimes like to think. In fact, sometimes the part about leaving the light on and accidentally electrocuting my sister is actually more real to me than the image I have of me standing on a box in the gray dawn and peering through the bathroom window at the old man lying there on the floor. It cuts deeper and hurts longer. Maybe because, real or not, I didn't exactly know the old man all that well, whereas my sister and I used to be so much alike. But that's funny too, because now, even though she just lives in Smithfield, we're not really that close any more, whereas, with the old man, when I picture myself looking through that window at him, I feel somehow bound to him in a way I can't even explain.

When I really think about it, I guess the reason the light bothered me so much anyway was because of the dream. And that's strange too, because I must have had that dream fifteen or twenty years ago. But there are things like that, things that just won't let go of you, like the way the cold and slightly musty air of November makes me think of finding the old man. That's how it is with the light: even though I was only about nine or ten or something like that when I had the dream, I still can't help feeling a little bit sick whenever I pass by a house in the middle of the night and see a light still burning in one of the back rooms. In the dream, I must have been the last one to go to bed and I must have left the hall light on too, because I remember, still in the dream, my mother waking me up, shaking me and crying that someone had left the light on, and my sister Karen must have gotten up in the middle of the night and touched the switch because now she was lying there dead—electrocuted—on the hall floor.

And I guess maybe that explains why I felt so uncomfortable when I woke up to go deer hunting early that November morning and saw the old man's light still burning next door. I had noticed it just before I went to bed and, to be honest, I'd even seen it and thought about it a time or two earlier in the evening. Anyway, there it was, at five-thirty in the morning, still on, and when I looked out and saw it, my stomach gave that funny little signal that tells me something is wrong. I didn't really know him—he'd only moved in about three weeks before—but we had shared a newspaper for a week or so. He took the *Salt Lake Tribune* and offered to stick it between the railings on his porch when he was finished. If I didn't pick it up, though, he wasn't likely to leave it out the next night. I had gone over to get it just about dusk and, when it wasn't there, I decided I'd have to check back later. It still wasn't there around nine or ten, so I stood there on the porch debating whether to knock or just let it go. I wasn't sure whether he had forgotten or was being obstinate. But there was a light burning somewhere in the back of the little house, so I finally knocked—once, or maybe even twice, but not too loud in case he was asleep—and when he didn't come, I went on back home. I think I looked out and saw the light still on before I went to bed, and I think I almost knew even then, but I didn't do anything. That's what bothers me. I reasoned it out that

177

he probably wasn't answering the door because he wasn't feeling well and had gone to bed early, but now I sometimes wonder why I didn't keep knocking or why I didn't knock louder. That's what makes me feel so terrible sometimes—because the next morning when I looked out and saw the light and when I finally went out and tried the door and then got a box and dragged it over to the little bathroom window where the light was still burning, I knew when I saw him there lying on the floor, dead from a heart attack, that maybe, sometime the night before, I might have done something and that now, like it or not, that old man and his death were linked to me forever.

I think about it a lot. Even a hazy gray morning or the smell of dry leaves, like I said, will bring it all back. And then sometimes too the dream about my sister gets mixed up in there somewhere and I start feeling twice as guilty. I don't think I ever even told her about it, which is kind of funny because we used to tell each other almost everything. She was just one year younger than I was, but the older we got the more she treated me like a big brother, asking me what she should wear and what she should do and so on. We were actually a lot alike. Even in elementary school, there were times when we almost avoided our own friends in order to continue some game she and I had been playing or finish a project we had started. It's funny how you think then that anything is possible, that the whole world is within reach and the only thing holding you back at all is your age. What dreamers we were!

There were a lot of places we used to go to make our secret plans —sometimes behind the lilac bushes and sometimes out under the plum trees—but most of all it was in a grove of cottonwoods on the edge of the pasture where the horses were kept. Five or six of the trees there had grown in a kind of ring, already close enough together and linked by an old log and enough fallen branches that it didn't take many trips up there to build a circular wall of twigs and boards that shut us off in a sort of lavender glow—not only from the rest of the pasture but, in fact, from the whole town. We found little niches there where we could stash our poems or drawings, and there was another hollow place, just big enough for one person, where I would sit and watch Karen twirling with scarves as she made up dances and acted out scenes from plays she made up herself. She used to do that a lot. In fact, she even went into Salt Lake on Saturdays to take ballet lessons—at least up until she was a junior or senior in high school. Anyway, we talked a lot in those days about Hollywood, New York, and San Francisco—places we'd never even seen, and still haven't, I guess, for that matter. She was supposed to become an actress or ballet dancer or both, and I was supposed to design all the costumes and scenery. I used to draw a lot then, and for a long time I kept a cigar box full of sketches and ideas; I don't know whatever happened to them. Things change and you forget about all that.

I sometimes wonder, though, how much Karen remembers. She's pretty busy, I know. Cliff's got a good job at Thiokol, and they've got a fairly nice home and five—well, almost six—kids now so she doesn't get down here much, and, because it's hard for me to leave the store, I really don't get up there either. But I wonder sometimes if she ever thinks much about our days here as kids, about the cabin we built in the loft of the Swensons' barn, about the time we chased the Starkie kids clear up on top of the Public Library, or about the Strangs or Stangers or whatever their name was.

Derryl Stanger. That's funny that I would even think of him, because I haven't really thought of him much for a long time. I do remember one thing though. The first time I saw him was on the Fourth of July when he was with his sister and their mother. I thought they must be visiting relatives, but somebody said, no, they were going to live here. And later on I found out he was in my class at Sunday School, and once or twice near the end of the summer we played together a little. But that fall we were in the fourth grade, and by the end of the first week, Mrs. Spendlove had us vote for who we wanted to be class president. I think we were supposed to fold our arms on our desks and then bury our heads while she asked for a raise of hands, but somebody in the class peeked because, even though Richie Cameron won, the word spread around during recess that Derryl Stanger had voted for one of the girls and we were all going to have to gang up and get him after school. I wonder now why I went with them; I never really liked Richie Cameron anyway. But we went after Derryl and caught him out behind the school building where he was getting on his bike, and when they all laid into him with their fists, I think I tried to hit once or twice too. I doubt if I really would have done it, but I saw Riley Shepherd gritting his teeth and kicking at the spokes of Derryl's bicycle—and Riley used to play with Derryl more than I did—so I didn't feel too bad, at the time.

The other thing I remember about that family actually had more to do with Karen than with me, because Derryl had a sister (whose name I don't even remember) who was Karen's age, and even before either one of us knew for sure who she was, Mama had invited her to Karen's birthday party on July 28th. But somehow someone must have gotten the message wrong because the party came and went and no one, I guess, even missed the little Stanger girl. But the next day, about two o'clock in the afternoon, there she was. The awful part was that she was not only dressed up in a new yellow party dress, but she was also wearing her own little crepe-paper party hat and held something—either a horn or a noisemaker of some kind— in one hand and a present wrapped with a bow in the other. I remember, because I was standing in the kitchen doorway, and I was as horrified to see the little girl there on the front porch as I was to see Karen push the door almost shut and come running toward me. What can I do, she wanted to know. And then Mama came from the other room, and when Karen told her, Mama said we'd just have to invite her in; there was still some ice cream left in the fridge. Karen was aghast: oh no, I couldn't, she said; I could never tell her. So Mama went to the door and Karen hid in her room, crying, and I was embarrassed too and didn't want to be in either place. But then, if I remember, Mama came back from the door with the present and said the little girl had gone home. The next day I saw where she had thrown the horn and party hat into a vacant lot.

I don't know whatever happened to the Stangers. I think they moved away after about a year. Like I said, I played with Derryl a few times, and I guess, in a way, we should have been good friends. But it never really happened. He collected post cards from around the world, I remember—and books on butterflies. The kids called him "Strategy."

There was a younger brother too, who I never really knew at all—except that he belonged to the family. He was about twelve by the time they moved, I guess, but the last thing I can remember about those kids at all has to do with him, and it was the Fourth of July again or at least some parade like that, and he was marching with the Boy Scouts. The only thing was, though, he was the only boy without a uniform. He just had on a little white T-shirt and some kind of pants, and I remember that he didn't really look up as he passed by, and I remember too how the whole thing made me feel kind of sick. Like I said, I really don't know whatever happened to any of them.

Anyway, I don't know if Karen remembers much about those days. And I don't know if things come back to haunt her the way they do me. With the kids and all, I'm sure she's plenty busy. I don't have a family, but, since Dad died, just running the store keeps me busy enough, I guess. It's funny how things go, though. I guess I kind of encouraged Cliff and Karen to get married because, by high school, he had become a pretty good friend of mine—his dad ran the church farm and mine had the only feed store around—and I guess at that time I had some kind of vision of all of us becoming one big happy family some way—I don't think I was ever sure how. We do get together for family reunions and things though.

There are a lot of memories that crowd into my mind at times. The worst ones, though, like I said, are the ones that were really just a dream—the one about the light switch, I mean—and then the other one—the one that really *did* happen a few years ago—about the old fellow next door. And like I said, even though the dream about my sister wasn't true, that didn't stop me from feeling pretty terrible about it for days after, and even now, sometimes, if I happen to see a light burning in the night. Of course, now it's mixed up with the memory of the old man on the floor in the doorway. But, do you want to know the funniest thing of all? Sometimes I start thinking that it wasn't a heart attack that killed the old man after all, but the light. And worse still, sometimes when I imagine myself looking through the window into that dingy little room with the single light still burning at five-thirty in the morning, I often get the same shivery feeling that the old man I'm looking at lying there on the rug is me.

The Wheelbarrow

It really had nothing to do with the chickens; yet, as he glanced back at them over his shoulder from where he stood in the peeling doorway of the back porch, one foot resting just inside the open screen door and the other still on the next to the last step, he watched their dingy-white bodies moving jerkily among the obstinate patches of last week's snow, and he felt he had to do something. Still, he didn't move. Despite the feeling that stirred restlessly inside him, squirming and pecking nervously like an unborn chick inside its shell, he remained transfixed, almost paralyzed.

"Your gravy's getting cold." It was Valene, her voice far away yet slicing across thought-years, cutting through layers of blurred memories to serve up an immediate hunk of now, cold and November-gray in the afternoon dusk.

A shudder rippled through his body and he prepared himself to move. Yet he didn't. He glanced back at the chickens instead, their heads twitching erratically as they pecked at unseen particles on the frozen ground, endlessly clucking to themselves. Beyond them by the leafless cottonwood, he could see the fence patched with wire and odd boards; the tub used for the horses' watering trough, clotted now with dead leaves and a jagged ring of ice; and, lodged against the bare, spidery branches of the lilac bushes, a rusted wheelbarrow, a crusty triangle of snow caught inside it.

He was aware of the numbness coming over him as he looked at the backyard, and it seemed to overtake him even more when he thought of the house, of the yellow-flowered wallpaper and the dark varnished woodwork and furniture waiting inside. It had been coming on for years, he knew that, yet there was something new and frightening, something almost physical, about the isolation

182

now; he was becoming detached, almost totally transported from the feel of the cement step beneath his foot or from the light and sounds coming from the kitchen.

He looked beyond the fence and the bare lilac bushes to the barn. It had been her backyard, after all, not his; he had never accepted this—never, really, even asked for it. His own childhood had had its share of backyards—an interminable blur of cropped lawns and painted swing sets tacked on to the temporary housing of air force bases from Elmendorf, Alaska, to Wright-Patterson, Ohio. None of these scenes begged him for sentiment, berated him for a lack of nostalgia; they turned, instead, their cold, indifferent backs. He, too, had never regretted their inevitable parting; even if he had disliked them on first sight, he was always assured that in a matter of months all would be different. He glanced at the chicken coop with its broken door propped shut by a stick, then at the woodpile under scraps of snow, and, further on, at the pitchfork leaning against the unpainted barn, a lopsided piece of rock salt lodged against the weathered wall in a crust of dirty snow.

I should feel something toward all this, he thought. *Even if it isn't mine, was never mine, it seems as if I'm supposed to feel something—maybe because it's something I should have had, or because it's something she once had and therefore should still have some meaning—* Something frightened the chickens and they scattered, fluttering and clucking nervously for an instant, then went back to pecking at the few grains sprinkled on the blackened earth. He looked at the wheelbarrow, at the stiff, dried bushes and watering trough. The cold afternoon light was failing and everything stood out sharply, without shadow or highlight, as if balanced, waiting on the edge of the world, about to tip forward or hurl itself suddenly into space.

How could she expect him to feel anything for Tropic, Utah, or for this house with its cold back bedroom and the awkward varnished dresser with the rippled mirror, for the barn or the chicken coop or any of these things in the backyard? His own memories meant little enough, he had to admit—except for random moments that persisted in haunting him like lines from an old song, moments when the keys of a piano had suddenly responded beneath his fingers in a surprising new chordal structure, or he had lost himself in the bluish glow while the sticks in his hands came alive against the drumskins and the cry of Bry Swenson's sax sailed cool and silver overhead.

"Hey, Valene's got your supper all dished up in here, Theron." Now it was his father-in-law, licking a daub of gravy from the corner of his mouth and waving a turkey bone from the doorway leading to the kitchen. Like his boys, Travis Myers came almost to the top of the door frame; and his dry, sparse hair, like theirs, seemed an extension of his speckled skin. The big man backed awkwardly into the lighted kitchen as Theron finally stepped inside the back porch, the screen door banging behind him, and moved among the milk cans, bridles, and washing machine to the room where his two brothers-in-law sat hunched over the table, their plates heaped with food, and his daughters, Kathy and Laurie, squirmed awkwardly on their chairs.

"But I don't feel like anything," Laurie whimpered, scrunching up her shoulders and pulling in her neck so that her cheek rubbed against the blue puffed sleeve of her Sunday dress. "Except pie." He noticed that her eyes were looking up at him, appealing for his aid.

"Me neither," Kathy announced quietly, sitting sideways on her chair and looking at the wall. She was almost seven, two years older than Laurie, six years older than the baby, Trisha. "Gol, we just barely ate."

"You hardly ate enough to keep a bird alive," his mother-in-law announced from the sink. She was not really a large woman, yet her hips swelled out enormously from her yellow apron.

"I'm stuffed," Laurie said emphatically. She glanced up at him, both of them, he thought, expecting to hear next about all the starving children in China. Garth mumbled something and Neldon laughed; they went on eating, still smirking under their freckles.

"Sit down," Valene scolded from the doorway leading into the hall, and he looked up to find that she was talking to him. From the way the receiving blanket was thrown across her shoulder and chest, he could tell she was nursing the baby; and he winced at how, though cradled in both her arms, it nevertheless seemed to be resting on the slight shelf of her protruding stomach, which, after seven months, had not completely gone down. Her hips, he noticed, were beginning more and more to flare out like her mother's.

Theron looked at the kitchen table where his father-in-law had already resettled himself and was now scraping a mass of the sweet potatoes onto his plate. A wave of the man's mottled head indicated that the vacant place next to him was Theron's. Warmed-over remnants of their earlier Thanksgiving dinner appeared wilted and uninteresting on the plate in front of the empty chair.

His mother-in-law motioned as if to take away the plate as he began to sit down. "Darn it, I'm afraid you've gone and let that get cold," she said.

"I was under the impression everyone was going to more or less fix his own—"

"I called him three times," Valene addressed the room, boosting the baby onto her shoulder and adjusting the blanket.

"Maybe I'll just have a little bit of this dressing anyway and a piece of cold—"

"You don't want any gravy? I thought you liked my gravy." His mother-in-law looked puzzled, hurt.

He refused to let her take the plate, jabbed at the warmed-over potatoes, tasted them half-heartedly. "They're okay. Fine," he lied.

He felt flushed. The room itself seemed overly warm, and under the yellow-bright light of the naked bulb overhead, with the shifting figures around him appearing only fuzzily, he felt as if he were in an incubator. Only a moment ago he had stood in the ice-blue light outside, feeling somewhat isolated, estranged; now he would welcome a chance to break from the stifling closeness of the kitchen to the liberating freshness of the air on the other side of the door.

"Now sit up in your seat and eat," Valene coached the girls from behind, joggling the baby on one shoulder now as she tried to turn Laurie around in her chair. Theron noticed how much they all seemed to resemble Travis: when he had married Valene nine years ago, he had thought of her as a somewhat pale but pretty girl with long hair the color of honey or a wheatfield (he had, in fact, pictured her during those days in a filmy white dress and wide-brimmed sun hat, photographed soft-focus, blowing a feathery dandelion—an impressionistic album cover for a record, frequent then in his imagination but never recorded, featuring his own jazz improvisations of Debussy's "Girl With the Flaxen Hair"); now, with her hair cropped boyishly short ("I couldn't stand all that hair on my neck," she had announced one summer) and having acquired a rusty tinge he had never remembered, once-unnoticed freckles seemed to have multiplied into countless brownish blotches, linking her finally, and unquestionably, to the big man and his two boys, vigorously chewing their food behind their speckled-trout complexions, seated at the table. And now, he noticed, the same rusty quality was not only there in Kathy and even in Laurie, but was there already, unmistakably, in Trisha as well, her fine baby hair and tiny eyebrows almost orange-gold against the vulnerable paleness of her skin.

He became aware of the squirming still going on inside him, and he grew anxious to finish his food and leave; still, something weighed him down, and even lifting his fork seemed an effort. Across from him, Laurie begrudgingly picked at something on her plate, then pushed it away and flopped back against her chair. She braced her skinned knees against the table and looked up at him from under her bangs, her blue eyes surprisingly like Valene's. He saw Neldon reach a rough hand across the table, his thumbnail a blue-black wedge, and tug at a lock of Kathy's sandy hair as she slumped sideways in her chair, stubbornly resisting Valene's proddings to eat.

"I'm gonna get me a blonde-headed girl," he sang chidingly, faking a Western twang and improvising a tuneless tune, " 'cause I'm tired of squeezin' blackheads."

Valene poked at him from behind as she hoisted the baby up on her hip and seemed to suppress a smile. "That's enough out of you," she said.

Theron found himself staring at Kathy's hair, remembering how Valene's had been, remembering the album cover and the record he had never made, the unfinished arrangements and scraps of original jazz melodies stuffed in folders and boxes collecting dust in one basement or another or piled high on the rafters of the landlord's garage. He couldn't account for the days, the years, that had slid somehow by him: it had been nine years—no, ten—since the last fall he had played drums with the BYU combo known as The Cool Touch, and almost thirteen years since he had been part of Jerry Eggleston's Mood-makers. For a moment he could almost hear Lori Ashby huskily singing "Misty" in the old June Christy style, her head tilted so that her long hair hung down to where her white hands cradled the microphone. Where had they all gone—Lori, Jerry, Bry Swenson on sax? Someone had mentioned once that they had run on to Lori in San Francisco or Sausalito— that she had married out of the Church, gone through a rather bitter divorce, and then—he wasn't sure what had happened then. For him she was still back there somewhere in 1960 cradling the mike and singing:

Look at me,
I'm as restless as a kitten up a tree . . .

"Pass me down a hunk of that homemade bread," Neldon mumbled, giving him a little nudge. "The heel there. Gimme the heel."

Theron reached for the plate.

"You pull up a chair and sit down there too, Valene," his mother-in-law was saying from the sink. "I can take the baby and burp her while you get a bite to eat. Dish yourself up some potatoes and some of that good gravy."

"Taters and gravy and dog's hind leg," Garth said, and he and Neldon both laughed.

He tried to remember if the word to the song was really *restless*. Or was it *lazy*? He tried to sing it over in his mind, and the notes, as Lori had sung them, came back to him:

Look at me,
I'm as—

But the word was blurred.

"Is it really dog's hind leg?" Laurie asked.

"Of course it isn't," Valene said, casting a fierce glance at Garth that failed to mask a smile. "Now sit up straight and eat, or you'll go to bed without anything."

He wanted to ask Valene, "Remember that song, 'Misty'?" and then ask her if she could remember the words, but he knew what she would say. It wasn't just that she was four years younger, or even that she had grown up spending more time listening to the Everly Brothers than to Stan Kenton or Dave Brubeck; what both- ered him most was her almost complete indifference to music at all. Aside from her off-tune attempts to sing nursery rhymes with Kathy and Laurie, the only song he could recall her paying any attention to at all within the past ten years was "I Never Promised You a Rose

187

Garden," and he had cringed every time he had heard her trying to sing along with Lynn Anderson from the little radio in the kitchen. Twelve years ago—even ten, maybe—the thought of marrying a nonmusical girl would have been incomprehensible to him. And actually, even after he met her, he had never thought of her as non-musical. She had liked to dance, and she had certainly expressed awe at his ability to play the drums. And when he had told her of his dreams to play with Cal Tjader or Vince Garaldi, she had listened wide-eyed and, as he remembered it, entranced. But the years since then had not been smooth; it wasn't right, he knew, to blame her that he had taken over a job teaching the fourth and fifth grades in a little school in Arizona or that he had eventually been sidetracked into selling mimeograph machines for a year and a half. She was not responsible either for what went wrong in Los Angeles when he had finally found a way to drift back into music, not responsible for their apartment with the turquoise and yellow wallpaper and the man that had shot his wife next door, for the smoky haze of nights-leading-into-mornings trying to beat out rhythms against the clatter and laughter of the clientele at The Cellar, for the quarrels with Tony, for the part-time job at The Cavern, for Dizzy's crack-up or the fiasco in Las Vegas, for the money they borrowed from Les and from her uncle in Sacramento, for any of it—even for finally returning to Utah and for the last three-and-a-half years selling vacuums for Sears in Price. And yet—

"Stop squirming!" It was Valene's voice, and he saw her pull Laurie back onto the seat of the chair. "Do you need to go to the bathroom or what?"

"You sit up and eat your supper," Valene's father was saying, motioning with the blade of his knife, "and I'll take you over to Henrieville tomorrow and show you some brand-new baby pigs." He went on chewing, watching her face as if waiting for a reaction. "And I might even be able to scare up a baby calf or two."

"I thought we were going to the hills to get a Christmas tree," Laurie said. She looked at Theron: "You said after Thanksgiving we could—"

He felt everyone's eyes on him. He wiped his mouth with a napkin and announced, somewhat weaker than he wanted, "That's right. I did promise." Then to her: "We'll see if we can find a little tree for Grandma and Grandpa and get it set up before we have to go back home." When he had first suggested going into the hills to look for a tree, it had been the day after their arrival, and as he looked out of the kitchen window to where the blue-gray bushes faded into the dark woods beyond, the idea had come to him as a way out, a means of escape from the warm closeness of the kitchen, from the clutter—the milk bottles, fruit jars, newspaper clippings, and grease-stained recipes on the linoleum-covered cabinet beside the sink, from the cans and bridles on the porch, from the backyard with its rusty wheelbarrow and clucking chickens. Later, he had forgotten about it; but now the thoughts of the cool dark woods pulled him, tugged at him. Yet he didn't move.

"I thought we were all going to spend the day at the church," Winnifred Myers said to her husband, her voice flat. "Here everybody's talking about Christmas trees and baby pigs, and you know darn well you told Brother Liston you'd be at the church to help."

"Help do what?" Kathy perked up.

"They're fixing up Grandma and Grandpa's church," Valene shushed her. "Now eat your dinner."

"And *we* get to help," Laurie announced, wide-eyed, to her sister.

" 'Course you can help," Valene's mother went on. "They've got plenty for everybody to do if we're going to get it finished for Sunday. I don't know what all this talk about going over to Henrieville is all—"

"Okay then—we'll go see the baby pigs another day," the old man said, waving a chunk of bread in the air. Theron listened for a note of bitterness, of defeat, but heard none.

"Will they let me paint? With a brush?" Laurie was sitting up straight now. He remembered one night, almost a year ago, when he had come home from work and found her painted up with Valene's lipstick and tangled up in one of her old formals. It was true that she had looked clownlike, yet beyond that had been a reflection of the old Valene, and he had turned on the radio and danced with her all through the house.

"Paint, no," he heard Valene say as she filled up Laurie's fork with peas and potatoes and gravy and waited to poke it in her mouth, "but you can probably help pick up things—nails and pieces of plaster or whatever. Here, open your mouth."

"Maybe Theron don't want to spend his vacation working on the church," Valene's mother announced, leaning over the table to rearrange serving bowls. She seemed to avoid his gaze, but he felt the remark was directed at him and he found his shoulders gradually pulling themselves into a shrug. His throat tried to find something to say even before he was sure what it would be, but Valene cut him off.

"That's the only way we'll get to see anybody," she said, looking at him directly, shaking her head slightly with emphasis. "Geneva said DeVere's been up there every day this week and if we're going to catch him at all, it'll probably have to be *there*. There's probably a lot of people home for holidays and we don't even know about it. Besides," she went on, buttering a piece of bread and putting it in Laurie's hand, "it *was* my chapel—for almost twenty years. I don't think it would hurt to—"

He let his shoulders relax and felt his hands make a little gesture. "Whatever," he said hoarsely, not sure what he meant. He tried to visualize the chapel and the changes that might be underway. Among the overalled men with their hammers and paint brushes, and the robust women scrubbing floors or varnishing benches, he envisioned himself slipping off for a moment into some neglected back room and discovering a piano under a dusty canvas. At the thought, his fingers seemed to uncurl and probe for imaginary keys along the edge of the table. It had been a long time; even a set of drumsticks might feel alien now. And yet—

On my own
Would I wander through this wonderland alone . . .

Somewhere beyond Neldon's voice and Garth's laugh he could still hear Lori Ashby singing softly to the microphone, Buddy Holland improvising on the piano, then Bry Swenson's lonely sax. What had happened to them all? The late hours practicing in the basement rooms of College Hall—what were they all for? Did they know then it was all leading toward this? Something ached inside, and he found himself pushing away the plate of potatoes and gravy, cold and half-eaten. Beyond the clatter of the dishes and the silverware he heard the cry of Bry's sax rising above the Shearing-like notes of the piano, the steady whisper of his brushes on the drums or the cymbal, and under it all the reverberating foundation of Rob Hadley's bass; the notes bounced now and echoed through his mind as they had done, Novembers ago, against the walls of the practice room in College Hall. Rob Hadley, blond and round-faced, plucking the strings of the big bass, now dead somewhere, or so he had heard, in Viet Nam. Rob had been different—always willing to squeeze in a rehearsal or a performance with them, but somehow not quite totally committed, at least not the way *he* had been, and the way he had always felt Bry and Buddy were. He could see himself alone at the piano, hour after hour working out new arrangements, searching for new forms, new melodies; there had been days—months—when his whole world had been that little practice room on lower campus or the ballrooms where, amidst the bluish glow and the crepe paper, he had played with Eggleston's Mood-Makers or, later, with The Cool Touch.

"You seen the way Peewee Simkins has got that old Plymouth of Deloy's fixed up?" Neldon's voice startled him, and he looked up but found the boy looking off somewhere between Valene and Garth. Valene was looking over her shoulder to where her mother stood jiggling the baby, and he could hear her saying something about Relief Society, bottling plums, and the Spiritual Living lesson.

Something pressed against his chest from within. He knew he shouldn't blame her. It had been the unexpected turn music had taken as much as anything—the dominance of rock, the sudden shift in dancing styles. And yet, he had often thought he could have made the transition. Blood, Sweat, and Tears seemed, at times, to have managed it. And if the old style of Shearing and Brubeck or the sound of Stan Kenton and Sauter-Finnegan had been drowned out in the blare of electric guitars, the moist clean notes of Debussy had always been there for those who listened. Had he, somewhere along the line, stopped listening? He tried to penetrate the string of smoke-filled nights in the bistros and clubs of L.A. At least he had been trying, feeling out, groping. Yet it was true that it hadn't worked out, wasn't it? He *had* felt that as much as she—hadn't he?

"Do you or don't you?" Valene was saying. The warm kitchen swirled for a moment, and he became aware of how bright the single globe was just above Valene's head as he looked up to see her standing across the table, thrusting toward him, on a saucer, a shriveled piece of khaki pumpkin pie, the top parched and cracked, the edges turned brown.

"Isn't there—isn't there any whipped cream left?" he managed.

"No," she said dryly. "But you don't really need it with this recipe anyway. It's that one from the Relief Society recipe book, remember?" Before he could think of what she expected him to answer, she had already gone on: "But I don't want to force you to eat it if you don't want it. Laurie'll certainly eat it—if she'll just finish up her potatoes and gravy first. And those peas." She put the plate of withered pie down near the center of the table and poked at Laurie's food with the child's fork.

"But I wanted whipped cream too," he heard Laurie whimper as she shrank back in her chair, her neck disappearing into her shoulders.

"You gonna play basketball with us?" Garth was asking him, suppressing a belch as he got up from the table.

"Oh, you boys and your basketball," Valene's mother murmured from across the room where she stood with the baby. "I should think you'd've had enough basketball for one day. Why don't you go down to the church and see if there's anything you can do to—"

"On Thanksgiving?" Neldon blurted.

"Oh, well, I guess that's right, but you can bet they'll be counting on you all day tomorrow and the next day—and no two ways about it."

He had started to rise, yet something seemed to hold him there. He watched Neldon lean back, stretch, then reach across the table with one big hand to take up two or three rolls left over from the dinner earlier. He saw him flip Kathy's ear as he went around the table and followed his brother out the back door. Then Theron, too, found himself rising, his legs heavy and slow to move, thinking how he would not go with the boys to play basketball (just as he had not gone with them earlier that day), yet thinking, nevertheless, how the time was right to leave the table, to follow them out to where it would be cooler and he would be able to walk in the night air and think more clearly. Passing through the back porch, he heard Valene calling something to him about a coat and Laurie asking again why they wouldn't let her help paint at the church; but he pushed on through the back door into the cold darkness where he stood on the steps and watched his breath escape in disappearing puffs of steam. He thought of the word *misty*, of Lori's voice again and of the song, and suddenly there was the word that had eluded him earlier:

Look at me,
I'm as helpless as a kitten up a tree . . .

He could hear the boys starting up the pickup around the side of the house and he heard through the blackness Neldon's voice shout, "You comin'?" He called back his answer, then watched the lights gradually disappear as the pickup backed up and pulled away. Restless, he thought of starting up through the darkness into the hills behind the house; he thought of jogging down the road toward the lights of town. Yet he only stood there, shivering, on the porch, his breath escaping into the night.

He was not sure what time it was during the night that he heard her say his name. He had lain there awake, thinking, for what had seemed like more than an hour and a half, and it was just after he felt his mind beginning to drift into that stupor hovering on the edge of sleep that he felt her pressing her fist against the small of his back and heard her say through her teeth, "Theron, that's driving me crazy!" He felt his body stiffen while his mind was still groping to decipher her words. He raised his head enough to say, "What's the matter?" without turning over to face her.

"I can't sleep with you drumming your fingers on the pillow or the mattress or whatever it is you're doing," he heard her say.

"I didn't even know I was doing it," he said, wondering if he really *had* known.

"Well, you've been beating out rhythms with your fingers on the mattress or something, and it was just about driving me crazy."

"Have you been awake all this time?" he asked.

"I think I've dozed off and on." She hesitated, but by her breathing he could tell she had something more to say. Then he heard her voice again, slow and dry: "I think we need to talk about something."

Everything was quiet for a moment. Thinking he needed to make some response, he managed to say, "What's that?" He realized

193

he had almost stopped breathing; he was aware of his heart pounding against the mattress. For months now something had been building inside him, growing and mounting until he knew that a confrontation was inevitable. Several times he had wanted to approach the subject; once or twice it had swelled inside him until he had wanted to blurt it out—yet something had always held him. Now it was seconds away from being expressed concretely: what surprised him was that it was Valene, not he, who was about to bring it up.

"I've decided something," she said.

He waited for her to go on, listening to her breathing behind his back. Compelled, he finally said, "What's that?" He would let *her* express it.

There was a pause, then: "I've felt for quite a while that maybe —well, that things are just not right. I don't know if you've felt that way but—"

He wanted to say, "Yes—yes, I have," yet the words wouldn't come out and he found himself letting her go on.

"Well, anyway—I think you know as well as I do that there's something you've been neglecting that—well—that you've just *got* to do, and maybe it's been partly my fault if—"

His mind raced ahead, not hearing her words. He didn't want her to take the blame; he didn't totally blame her himself. Along with her unflagging sense of duty there had always been a touch of the martyr—something he admired as much as despised. But taking the blame was not the answer, not what he was seeking; he didn't want a settlement, a compromise, he realized now. He was afraid it was going to have to be more final than that, more complete—and he knew that now as he had known it for a long time, realizing that only the existence of the children had stalled him, prolonging what must have always been and what seemed now, even more, so hopelessly inevitable.

"—and Mama feels just like I do," she was saying, "that you've just got to have support—"

No, he wanted to say, *it's too late for your support*, knowing that what was wrong and had been wrong from the first was something deeper than support, something he couldn't label or even begin to identify without wading back through the clutter of varied backgrounds and mixed interests, of common goals and private dreams, yet knowing as he thought it that the dream—

"—and so, anyway, that's how I feel," Valene was saying. "You've just *got* to help me."

There was something he had missed. He waited, trying to sort out what she had been saying, then heard himself asking shakily, "How do you mean?"

"With the girls," she said. "I've just got to have your support in disciplining them. You saw how they were tonight. It doesn't matter how patient I try to be or whether I end up scolding them and—"

Stop, he wanted to say. Somewhere something had gone wrong. Only seconds ago he had almost been holding his breath as he felt her moving them toward some frightening yet inevitable brink, but suddenly the precipice had been pulled away, and in its place, with a new horror all its own, he could see only a cold and rocky plateau stretching on and on forever . . .

"In L.A.," she went on, "it was different. I bore up because it seemed like you were never there, day or night, and I *had* to do all the disciplining and everything, but now that you've got a decent job and things are different, you've got to give me some kind of support. Mama feels like I do that if you would just fulfill your role as patriarch of the family—"

No, he thought, wanting either to curl up in a ball or writhe with the emptiness that ached inside him. *It isn't enough*, he thought, realizing now he was talking aloud, his voice breaking the silence like a faraway cry for help. Kneeling together occasionally in family prayer or circled around the fireplace on Family Night—it wasn't enough. The Kool-Aid and popcorn, the little Primary songs they all tried to sing together, the tedious games of "Hide the Thimble" and "Old Maid"—how could she ever understand that for him they were not, and would never be, enough?

He was startled by a cry from another room. Valene shifted; then, as the cry came again, she sat up in bed. "It's Laurie—having another nightmare," she mumbled, flinging back the heavy quilts and getting up. He heard her fumbling for her bathrobe, then saw her disappear through the doorway and into the hall where a light burned feebly. He didn't move, but kept his fists clenched, his elbows pressed tight against his stomach as if to confine there the

195

knot of pain that struggled to swell, maybe even to burst, in the hollow center of his being. He thought of Valene sitting by the makeshift bed in the front room where they had put the girls; he could picture her smoothing her hand over Laurie's forehead and telling her it was only a dream. Who was there to come to tell *him* that this too had all been a dream, that the nightmare was finally over and that now, at last, everything was going to be all right?

When he was little, thoughts of death had terrified him. He remembered the nights he had lain wide-eyed in the bed, afraid that first sleep and then death would overtake him if he let his eyelids close. A boy his age had died of polio on the base at Lackland, and the staggering knowledge that even children could die had plunged him for months into a dark whirlpool; each night when the light in his room was turned off, he had lain there in terror, his mind whirling toward some black and awful vortex beyond which was only a soundless void. He thought about the year he had turned eleven, remembering the string of evenings in late spring when the missionaries in their white shirts and ties had always eaten with them and then stayed to help wash the dishes and talk of how life went on after death. He remembered how much easier going to bed had been after that, and he remembered going down under the water in the big, tiled baptismal font in Dayton, Ohio, and how the old fear had somehow been washed away. But he winced with pain even now, recalling the day two years later when his father had packed up and moved into quarters of his own, and he and his mother had gone first of all to Birmingham, then to Columbus, and finally to Bakersfield, California, where he finished high school. He tried now to remember those days, but they seemed somehow blocked off, barred from memory. There were moments—sounds, pictures—that crept through: marching across the football field with the snare drum rubbing against his blue and gold uniform, listening to an old recording of *Vesti la Giubba* for the first time one winter afternoon in a chorus class, suddenly wondering if a certain pattern of notes picked out on the music room piano was inspired or borrowed. But what came back to him most of all was something sheared of sound, shunning images; it was more than anything a feeling—gray like loneliness, hollow like hunger. If the old fear of death had subsided somewhat after the missionaries, then his parents' divorce, it occurred to him now, had awakened in him a new and yet related fear; it was as though he had stepped out of a parade to tighten his drum or pick up a lost stick and when he hurried back to find his place, the uniforms were not the same and he couldn't recognize the cadence. He had often dreamed, in fact, that he was hurrying along a ravine or that he had somehow slid down an embankment; it was always dusk and against the horizon he could see the reflected glow of lights where music—gay yet far-away like that of a distant carousel—seemed to be playing. It was as if he knew the carnival was closing up or being taken down and that he had to hurry or it would be gone; yet he could never find the end of the ravine, and every time he tried to climb up the side of the embankment, it only gave way and crumbled, and he would run along looking desperately for a better place to get out, but then the music would wind down and the lights would fade; and he would wake up, sweating and shaking against the cold sheets.

He turned over now, hoping that his thinking about the dream would not bring it on when he did finally fall asleep. He waited for a sound in the hall that would tell him that Valene, with Laurie consoled and sleeping now, was on her way back to bed. He felt nervous; his legs and fingers twitched. Yet when he did see her silhouette suddenly filling the doorway and hesitating there, he closed his eyes and tried breathing deeply and steadily in order that she might think he had fallen asleep. When he half-opened his eyes again, he realized that the light was coming through the doorway unimpeded now, yet she had never come back to the bed. He raised himself up on one elbow and looked around the darkened room, but he could tell it was empty.

Lying back against the pillow, he tried to think why he had feigned sleep. He tried to remember what she had been saying before Laurie's cry and what she might have wanted to say when she came back. He closed his eyes again, relieved that she had not come back to bed, yet his eyes opened almost against his will, and he found himself staring into the shadows overhead, wondering what the next step had to be, and, realizing that he knew that step, wondering if he would be able to take it. He suddenly became aware of people talking, faint and muffled, somewhere down the hall. He held his breath, trying to make out voices, words, but could distinguish nothing. He lay still for a moment, then, curious, got up carefully and crept to the door. The hall was empty, its faded flowered wallpaper yellow in the dim light of the funny little fixture hanging overhead. He waited. The voices went on, but still he caught no words, no meaning. Through the door across the hall he could see into the front room where, under the heap of patchwork quilts and knitted afghans, Kathy and Laurie were sprawled out on the feather ticks that had been temporarily arranged on the circular rag rug. Nearer the doorway he could make out the plaid car bed and the flannel blanket rising and falling with Trisha's even breathing. The door to the boys' room was closed, and midway down the hall the bathroom appeared dark; next to it, the door ajar yet giving no indication of light, was the room where Travis and Winnifred Myers slept. Despite the darkness, the voices, he could tell, were coming from there. He hesitated a moment, then slipped quietly down the hall, stopping momentarily in front of the bathroom door, then moving closer to the door, partly opened, a few feet beyond.

"—felt it would be so much better once we got out of that rotten environment," Valene was saying, "but now I just feel like he doesn't even try to understand—"

"Well," he heard her mother say, keeping her voice low, "you've just got to go to the bishop, that's all there is to it. Do you want to go talk to Rulon Liston while you're here, see what he has to say? You remember him, don't you?"

"It's not really that bad," Valene's voice cut in. "I mean we're not about to get a divorce or anything—"

"Of course not," her mother said.

"—but it's just that I always felt that if we got married in the temple and did all the things we're supposed to do that everything would somehow—"

His mind raced, remembering the painful days of dating when marriage, to him too, had seemed a kind of vague yet indisputable answer.

"Well, you've just got to keep after him, being the best wife you can, encouraging him to get to his priesthood meetings and—"

"I do, I do," he heard Valene break in, "but he just seems to resent it. He's not really antagonistic or anything like that, but—"

"Well, you can just thank your lucky stars he's not like Bertie

198

Cloward's man. She can't even get him out once a year to the ward dinner, let alone to sacrament meetings. Bertie says he reads all that trash about horoscopes and astronomy—or whatever it is—and he's always finding something or other to argue with her about, whether it's predestination or some other fool thing."

"Theron's not like that," Valene said. "I think he believes in the church and everything, but—"

A scene flashed in his mind, and for a second he heard his mother's voice, as he had heard it the summer before, standing beside her outside the motel she and Smitty managed in Reno: *Do you go to church?*

He had hesitated. *Yes,* he had said finally, feeling somehow guilty even though the answer was true. *Do you?* he had then asked, retaliating.

He remembered how she had looked at him, then glanced away, fidgeting with her hair. *Not—not regularly. It just seems we're always so—so tied up here at the motel.*

"I always said," he heard Valene's mother going on, "that if you're attending all your meetings and doing all the things you're supposed to, you just don't have time to get off on the wrong track. That's the trouble with Garth. If he'd been working on the church last weekend like he should've, instead of traipsing all over looking for someone to play basketball with, he never would've run the pickup into the side of Erna Nielson's car."

There was silence, then he heard Valene say, "Well—I decided last winter that maybe if I read the scriptures every night—at least for a little while—and always made sure that we had family prayer and all that—"

"Well, I think you've done just grand," her mother cut in, "considering the lack of support he gives you. That little Laurie can rattle off the blessing on the food like nobody's business, and the way Kathy—"

"It's just that I want Theron to be enthused too—and dedicated—"

"The only thing Garth or Neldon either one is dedicated to is playing basketball or hunting jack rabbits. Or fooling with cars and trucks and whatever else they can take apart." There was a pause. "Theron, now—you'd think he'd want to be just as good an example as he can to those little girls. Don't he have any goals? Don't he want to make his life just as—"

"He works hard," Valene's voice said. "There were only two people in our whole area that sold more vacuums than he did a couple of months ago. And I don't want to give you the impression that he doesn't go to church—"

"Of course he goes to church," her mother cut in. "I don't doubt that for a minute." Again there was a pause. "He's not fooling around with those rock and roll groups again, though, is he?"

"No. He hasn't even touched his drums for three years. Anyway, it wasn't rock and roll."

"Well, it's just the greatest blessing in the world that you got him out of that awful environment down there in L.A. when you did. Daddy and me just worried ourselves sick every minute you was there. I don't think I slept a wink the whole time."

Something twitched and convulsed between his shoulders, and he leaned back quietly against the wall. His head had begun to ache and his legs felt unsteady. It was not true—at least not totally true—that Valene had forced him to come back to Utah. He had known that L.A. was not "the thing"—had known it after the first week and had come to know it more and more as each dingy night dragged on into each smoky dawn, the drumsticks almost working themselves mechanically in his numb hands. Yet there had been moments: once he had improvised on "I'm Always Chasing Rainbows," and the crowd had been right and everything had somehow clicked; and one afternoon he and Dizzy had been alone at The Cellar—he at the piano and Dizzy on trumpet—and they had improvised on some classical themes and tried some of his own things. Once in Las Vegas, too, when he had worked with Tony's combo, there had been one Saturday afternoon when they had experimented with his arrangement of Gershwin's *Rhapsody in Blue*, and for a long time, maybe even an hour, everything had fallen into place. He had felt that continual tingle down his spine, and it had seemed that he and the piano and Tony and Rusty and Lino Capua were all floating about twelve feet off the floor.

But Las Vegas had not been "the thing" either. Neither BYU nor Las Vegas nor L.A. But it was still out there somewhere; sometimes he didn't think about it, and sometimes, lately, it was almost as if he had forgotten it completely, and yet, somehow, he knew that it was always there, out there somewhere. The sound of his own breathing startled him suddenly, and he realized that he felt almost out of breath, his lungs burning, as if he had been running for a long time.

"—got to stick to what you believe in, what you know is right," Valene's mother was reinforcing.

"I know that. I just want to make *him* see what's really important."

"Endure to the end, that's all you can do. But you've got to let him know what you expect. No matter how you look at it, your happiness—and the girls'—is going to depend a whole lot on whether he's in there pitching with you or pulling against you. You've got to let him know right out what it is that's going to make you happy because there's not a single thing in this world worse than—"

He felt himself turning away, moving silently, numbly, down the hall, the headache spreading between his eyes and behind his ears. In the darkened bedroom he lowered himself down on the bed and fell back, drained, against the sheets, pulling the covers up over him. Once he had lain in bed trembling that death might overtake him if he slept; now the possibility seemed inviting. It was not exactly that he welcomed it; it was simply that he found he no longer cared.

The light was still dusky-dark when he awoke the next morning, one side of his body cold where the covers had been pulled away, and the other one warm where the sleeping figure curled against him. He lay still for a moment, waiting for the feeling of the night before to rush whirlingly upon him, but then he realized it had never left. The same numbness was upon him now, undiminished by sleep. He felt lifeless, yet his mind was clear: he knew what he had to do.

He moved to get up while the light outside was still blue-gray, taking care not to wake Valene, but as he rolled away from the warm cheek resting against his shoulder, he could feel the figure stir.

"Daddy?" The voice, thick with sleep, startled him. He looked and saw that it was Laurie beside him, her eyes flickering open and then closed, her sandy hair stuck damply to her cheek.

He sat up, glanced at Valene's side of the bed where the covers lay rumpled yet flat, then leaned over on one elbow to smooth the hair from Laurie's forehead. "Go back to sleep," he said quietly. His hand was shaking. "It's not really morning yet." She shifted down under the covers without opening her eyes, locking his hand between her warm, moist cheek and the cold sheets. He hesitated a moment, then carefully slid it out. He saw Laurie's eyes blink then close as she turned her face away.

The room was cold. He dressed quickly, his whole body shaking. Through the doorway he could see Valene curled up on one of the feather ticks where she had probably fled when Laurie had squeezed in beside them during the night. A twinge of guilt caused his shoulders to flinch; he didn't like to think about the nights—so many now it hurt to recall them—that he had lain in their bed in L.A. or in Price and let her attend to the girls' coughs and bad dreams. He had intended, in the old days, to take turns; yet, more and more, something had been weighing him down, walling him off, until that other world, the world of cough medicines and lunch money and buying new school shoes, had begun to seem like something apart, something muffled and only dimly seen as if from within the fuzzy walls of a cocoon. From the frosty window he could see the backyard: everything was touched with a silver-blue light; everything was still, waiting. He put on his coat and scarf, then his rubbers. His gloves were on the dresser where the starched doily didn't quite cover the stains—little circles, bleached white—on the dark varnished wood, where drops of rubbing alcohol or maybe hydrogen peroxide had spilled long ago. He rubbed his finger over one of the spots before picking up his gloves; he could almost make it disappear. It was strange, the feeling that rippled through him: once he had found this dark, glossy, outdated piece of furniture almost repulsive; and when they had arrived this week— could it really have been only two days ago?—and moved their bags into this cold back bedroom that had once been Valene's and her older sister's, he had looked at the dresser and thought how someone who cared about such things might come across it one day, strip it back to its natural wood and refinish it. Yet now, as he smoothed his fingers across its surface in the early morning light, he was strangely experiencing what seemed to be a third feeling. Maybe, he thought, it was because he was turning his back on it, because he was walking away from it forever, that it seemed now to exude a certain quaint charm, even in its ugliness, that he hadn't noticed before. He glanced through the yellowed lace curtains to the bare trees against the back fence and on toward the barn and hills beyond; he would have to hurry, for the light was changing rapidly.

Running the brush quickly and nervously through his hair in front of the warped mirror of the dresser, he imagined he could hear various creakings and stirrings coming from one room or another in the house, yet when he stopped and listened or looked out into the hall or, beyond, into the dimness of the front room, the house seemed still to be sleeping. But when he finally touched the door and started to slip through it, he glanced back at Laurie and saw her sitting up in the bed.

"Daddy," she called out, her voice matching the worry on her face, "where are you going?"

He put a finger quickly to his lips to quiet her, but before he could put together an answer, she had scurried out of the bed and flung herself around his waist. "Don't go without me," she pleaded, her face revealing an incredulity akin to what he felt rising up within him.

"Laurie," he heard himself say, trying to keep his voice low, "I was just going outside—for a little walk."

"Without me?" she asked. "Were you going for the tree without me?"

The tree. He had not thought of it since the night before at the table. He looked out through the curtains to the gray lace of the trees against the smoke-blue sky. The sun was not up yet, and the hills beyond were still lost in a lavender haze.

"It's still not quite morning," he tried to reason. "I'm just going out back to walk—"

"I'm coming too," she said, and dropped down on her knees beside an open suitcase and started pulling things out.

He felt weak. As she clumsily pulled on her tights and then a bulky sweater, the dusky woods outside kept luring his gaze through the lace curtains and beyond, and he could feel his grip tightening around the gloves in his hand.

"I need you to tie my shoes, Daddy," Laurie reminded him, "and you need to help me on with my boots too."

He could feel the numbness coming back into his arms, into his hands and fingers, as he knelt down and mechanically tied her shoes and then helped her push each foot into the white rubber boots Kathy had outgrown. He felt as if the hair were standing up on the back of his neck, and he realized he was shivering despite his heavy coat and woolen scarf. A creaking sound came from somewhere in the house, but when at last he took her hand and slipped through the doorway and then through the dim kitchen and the dark porch smelling of bridles and spilled milk, he took the saw down from its nail, opened the back door, and led her out into the silver frost of the premorning air, leaving the sleeping house behind.

Something stopped him as he started down the steps. "What is it, Daddy?" he heard her ask, feeling her hand tightening around his.

"I don't know," he said, hearing his own voice remote and far away, and realizing that he was telling her the truth. "Look at how everything is," he finally heard himself say. The same scene, he remembered had stopped him the evening before. Except for the sparkling layer of frost covering everything, it remained almost the same, untouched—the irregular bone-white fence, the dark pattern of branches crisscrossing in front of it, the startling red-orange of the wheelbarrow, and the three white chickens already pecking at the deep brown patches between the ragged scraps of snow—each item jutting away from the bluish-gray backdrop of the dark hills beyond, as if, like the gingerbread children in the fairy tale, they too had once been alive and now, enchanted, were only waiting under the sprinkling of frost to be released into life again. He felt a little shiver, as though the scene were begging for some kind of musical expression. Something like Erik Satie might have written, or Debussy or Ravel. He could imagine a flute—and a harp. Maybe even an oboe.

Laurie tugged at his hand. "Which way, Daddy?"

"I'm not sure," he said, almost whispering. He looked off toward the trees along the hill, then let his gaze drift back to the frosted fence and the wheelbarrow. As if following his eyes, she cried out,

"Can we take it, Dad? We can, can't we? We can bring the tree back in the wheelbarrow!"

He meant to tell her that it might be too old, that the wheel probably would not even work, that it would be too heavy and awkward to take into the hills, but she was already running to it and kicking at where the wheel was frozen into the snow and earth. He helped her pry it loose, his numb arms still working mechanically, and then knocked loose the snow-crusted triangle of dirty water and leaves frozen inside. And as they pushed it alongside the back fence and through the creaking gate beneath the old cottonwood, he looked up to see a dark bird fluttering its wings in the jagged branches overhead, sending down a crusty sprinkle of snow.

Something tingled along his spine and the backs of his arms as he pushed the wheelbarrow uphill. He felt awkward, uneasy; the wheel creaked and rubbed on one side, the saw bounced and rattled in the wheelbarrow, and he found it difficult not to step on the heels of Laurie's boots for she had ducked under his arm to help him grasp the handles of the wheelbarrow, her mittened hands now next to his, and he almost had to straddle her as they plodded together through the crunchy snow beneath the trees. It had been a long time, he realized, since they had walked together at all, yet there was something not wholly uncomfortable or unpleasant in the tingling sensation along his shoulders, back, and arms. He looked around him, the quiet trees standing out, silver-frosted, against the cool mist-blue of the early morning, and then he stopped.

"Daddy," he heard Laurie's voice chiding, becoming aware at the same time that her mittens had closed down tightly over his gloves and she was twisting her head around to look up at him in a nose-wrinkling smile. "How come you keep wiggling your fingers like that? You're playing the wheelbarrow just like a piano!"

His fingers, he realized, were now still, yet he was also aware that they felt nervous, eager.

"Can we have us a piano someday, Daddy? For our very own?"

He squatted down to her level and looked into her eyes without answering. How could he tell her now that there would never be a piano, that there would never, in fact, even be a "someday" for the five of them? He took off one glove and rubbed the backs of his fingers against the coolness of her cheek. He touched her eyebrow gently, then smoothed back a wisp of her hair that had strayed across her forehead. Her eyes—waiting, wondering—seemed to be studying his. He looked at them now, struck by their blueness—a silvery blue that was startling like the morning and the woods and the backyard covered with frost.

"Can we, Daddy?" he could hear her saying, but he was listening for other sounds, other notes. His fingers were twitching almost uncontrollably, and he found that, to steady himself, his hands had slipped down around her shoulders and were holding her frail arms through the heavy wool of her coat. Nervously, he glanced away for a moment to where the shadows waited in the woods beyond, still lavender and dark. A fine snow seemed to be falling now. He could feel her eyes, puzzled and waiting, but his gaze slipped past her to the wheelbarrow in the snow, and, behind it, their own tracks leading down through the trees to the farmhouse below. He tipped his head back, searching the whitening sky, his lungs contracting almost convulsively in the cold air, his eyes stinging with the flakes of snow.

"I don't know," he heard himself whisper. Then, hoarsely: "Maybe." The old pain was there again inside him, but still he didn't move. He could feel his hands tightening around her arms and he pulled her close to him, pressing his forehead against her woolen coat.

And for a long time, they stayed like that in the little clearing between the farmhouse and the woods—the child, shivering but unmoving; the father's shoulders shaking uncontrollably, shamelessly—beside the rusty wheelbarrow in the snow.